Spiritual Intimacy

Spiritual Intimacy

RICHARD MAYHUE

While this book is intended for the reader's personal enjoyment and profit, it is also intended for group study. A leader's guide with Reproducible Response Sheets is available from your local bookstore or from the publisher.

VICTOR BOOKS®

A DIVISION OF SCRIPTURE PRESS PUBLICATIONS INC.
USA CANADA ENGLAND

Library of Congress Cataloging-in-Publication Data

Mayhue, Richard.
    Spiritual intimacy / by Richard Mayhue.
       p.   cm.
    Includes bibliographical references.
    ISBN 0-89693-815-8
    1. Spiritual life. 2. Christian life—1960-   I. Title
BV4501.2.M428   1990   90-36997
248—dc20   CIP

CONTENTS

**To
Lee and Wade
with a father's prayer
that you passionately pursue
a growing intimacy with God.
2 Peter 3:18**

Whom have I in heaven but Thee?
And besides Thee, I desire nothing on
earth. My flesh and my heart may
fail, but God is the strength of
my heart and my portion forever.
Psalm 73:25-26

INTRODUCTION

"As the deer pants for the water brooks, so my soul pants for Thee, O God" (Ps. 42:1). The psalmist yearned for God with the same intensity as the publican who cried out, "God, be merciful to me, the sinner!" (Luke 18:13)—though each had a different reason.

One sought for a deeper relationship; the other, a new relationship. But both cried out for spiritual intimacy with God. Perhaps you can identify with one of them.

Augustine wrote in *The City of God,* "There is a God-shaped vacuum in every man that only Christ can fill."[1] That's where spiritual intimacy begins but it is by no means where it ends. It extends on in time and maturity until: we become God's friend like Abraham (James 2:23); we walk with God like Enoch (Gen. 5:22, 24); we enjoy intimate fellowship with God as did Job (Job 29:4, NIV); we, like David, grow into a man or woman after God's own heart (Acts 13:22, KJV); we know the high esteem of God similar to Daniel (Dan.

10:11, 19); or become a favored one of God like Mary (Luke 1:28). Just like them, we have the treasured opportunity to become "intimates of God."

Defining Intimacy

An intimate relationship is marked by very close association, contact, or familiarity. Expanding on that, an intimate friendship includes warmth, tenderness, love, closeness, transparency, security, vulnerability, strength, commitment, knowledge, and understanding.

Our chaotic world breeds a brutal, self-seeking attitude devoid of intimacy. That is why marriages crumble, families disintegrate, and friendships fail. To a world that callously disregards even the dignity of human life, God calls out with a word of love (John 3:16; Rom. 5:8) and beckons us to become intimate with Him.

In our "liberated" day, the intimate act of marriage has degenerated into cheap sex, both in and out of marriage. Mothers regularly kill their babies through abortion and children increasingly rebel against their parents in homes where family intimacy has long ago been abandoned. By ignoring God, society emotionally starves itself to death while all along God promises to love us forever and give us our fill of spiritual affection.

We live under continual threat of nuclear holocaust and experience daily, life-threatening violence. Newspaper headlines fill our minds with thoughts of euthanasia, infanticide, and genocide. These barbaric vulgarities can only be neutralized by spiritual intimacy with a compassionate God who alone can do all things and never fails. Our generation's greatest need is to reclaim a dominant sense of intimacy with God which will reshape our souls and redirect our lives.

Portraits of Love

For most of us, the thought of being intimate with God defies our understanding since He is God and we, mere humans. So

God in His Word uses three illustrations to help us understand the intimacy He desires with us.

A shepherd with his sheep. So close and so loving is the good shepherd to his flock that he is willing to die for their well-being (John 10:11). When the sheep hear the shepherd's voice, they know it well and follow him (vv. 4, 16, 27).

A man and his wife. Nearer to most people's experience is the picture of marriage. God the Father stands as Israel's husband (Isa. 54:5; Jer. 31:32) and Christ serves as the bridegroom for His beloved church (Eph. 5:25-32). With everlasting love and covenant faithfulness, the Lord intimately bestows His grace upon those who are His through faith in Christ.

A parent-child relationship. God is our Heavenly Father. As His redeemed children, it is our unique privilege to experience the depth of His love and call Him by the most intimate of endearments—*Abba,* the Aramaic equivalent for "Daddy" (Rom. 8:15; Gal. 4:6). In Christ we become little children (Matt. 18:3; 1 John 2:1). God knows us to the uttermost detail (Ps. 139:13-16) and reveals Himself in a knowing relationship that goes far beyond information—so far beyond that it results in eternal transformation (2 Cor. 3:18; Phil. 3:21; 1 John 3:2).

To balance out our thinking, we must not forget that a tension should always exist between responding in awe to the King of kings and coming in love to our Heavenly Father. Too much emphasis on kingship robs us of intimacy while excess attention to our family privilege leads us to presumption. Our relationship with God must always be kept in focus as one between the human and the divine.

Our Pilgrimage
Does this confession sound familiar?

As a young man I must have tried a dozen techniques that people said were sure to guarantee a measure of passion that would transport me above the ordinary and ineffective. In each case I eagerly embraced whatever it was that I was supposed to do or say. But the results, if any, were short-lived, and what I discovered was that there are no short-cuts, no gimmicks, no easy ways to cultivate an intimacy with God and attain the resulting passion that should carry one through life's journey.[2]

Spiritual Intimacy does not propose a "formula" approach to closeness with God. Rather, by coming to God through His Word, we seek to dynamically be and do those things which promote a holy environment for fellowship with Him. It's both a lifetime commitment and a spiritual style of living.

Listen to the Prophet Micah: "He has told you, O man, what is good; and what does the Lord require of you but to do justice, to love kindness, and to walk humbly with your God" (Micah 6:8).

In some sense, we follow by analogy the advice of John Wooden, the successful former basketball coach at UCLA. When asked by a reporter to explain his success, Wooden replied, "I merely taught my players to master the fundamentals."

Our study in this book is all about the fundamentals of spiritual intimacy with God. By God's grace, in Christ as a new creation, and through the Holy Spirit's power, we can "master the fundamentals." It must be our consuming passion to so highly prize God that we diligently cultivate His friendship and love.

God's Grace

Whether you rebel against God like the prodigal son (Luke 15:11-32), sincerely seek to know God like Cornelius and his family (Acts 10:1-2), commit sin and interrupt your intimacy like David (Ps. 51), or desire to reach a new level of communion with God like Paul (Phil. 3:12-14), these basics in building a growing, personal relationship with God will guide and equip you to satisfy your longings.

I pray that your spiritual journey and mine will be marked by the psalmist's childlike confidence in his side-by-side walk through life with God.

> *The Lord is my shepherd, I shall lack nothing.*
> *He makes me lie down in green pastures,*
> *He leads me beside quiet waters, He restores my soul.*
> *He guides me in paths of righteousness for His name's sake.*
> *Even though I walk through the valley of the shadow of death,*
> *I will fear no evil, for You are with me;*
> *Your rod and Your staff, they comfort me.*
> *You prepare a table before me in the presence of my enemies.*
> *You anoint my head with oil; my cup overflows.*
> *Surely goodness and love will follow me all the days of my life,*
> *and I will dwell in the house of the Lord forever.*
>
> Psalm 23:1-6, NIV

* * * * *

If you are interested in other books on this general topic, I recommend the following:

Jerry Bridges. *The Pursuit of Holiness.* NavPress.

W. Bingham Hunter. *The God Who Hears.* InterVarsity Press.

John MacArthur, Jr. *The Ultimate Priority.* Moody Press.

Richard Mayhue. *A Christian's Survival Guide.* Victor Books.

A.W. Tozer. *The Pursuit of God.* Horizon Books.

STEP ONE

"GETTING ACQUAINTED"

*Therefore if any man is in Christ, he is
a new creature; the old things passed
away; behold, new things have come.
2 Corinthians 5:17*

*Wherever there is joy in the world,
wherever there is hope, wherever there
is a spirit of moral victory, I find behind
it evangelical believers for whom God has
become personally real in their lives.*[1]
Carl F.H. Henry

Search me, O God, and know my heart;
Try me and know my anxious thoughts;
And see if there be any hurtful way in me,
And lead me in the everlasting way.
Psalm 139:23-24

1
KNOWING GOD

Record-setting Los Angeles Dodgers pitcher Orel Hershiser recalled the occasion when entertainer Frank Sinatra gave him and his wife, Jamie, an autographed photo:

"He signed it, 'To my great friends,' and he spelled our names, 'Oral and Jane.' Goes to show you how good of friends we really were."[1]

On a human level, Orel's story portrays the extent to which many think they can know God. Casually at best, and details just don't matter. However, that does not represent what the Bible teaches about knowing God.

God desires that we know Him intimately and that He knows us in the closest possible spiritual relationship. God issues this invitation to all: "Cease striving and know that I am God" (Ps. 46:10).

A.W. Tozer explains that either we can know the facts about God or we can enter into a personal relationship with God and even develop a deep intimacy with Him.

You and I are in little (our sins excepted) what God is in large. Being made in His image we have within us the capacity to know Him. In our sins we lack only the power. The moment the Spirit has quickened us to life in regeneration our whole being senses its kinship to God and leaps up in joyous recognition. That is the heavenly birth without which we cannot see the kingdom of God. It is, however, not an end, but an inception, for now begins the glorious pursuit, the heart's happy exploration of the infinite riches of the Godhead. . . .

To have found God and still to pursue Him is the soul's paradox of love, scorned indeed by the too-easily satisfied religionist, but justified in happy experience by the children of the burning heart.[2]

For a few, this discussion raises a fundamentally important question . . .

Is There a God to Know?

Col. James Irwin, *Apollo 15* astronaut, tells this true story concerning Yuri Gagarin, the first Russian cosmonaut. Gagarin sarcastically commented upon his return to earth that he did not see God in space. The implication—God does not exist.

A young Russian girl heard about the remark and wrote Yuri a letter. She asked, "Are you pure in heart? For if you are, you would have seen God." She drew her conclusions from Matthew 5:8, "Blessed are the pure in heart, for they shall see God."

Significantly, the Bible never proves the existence of God. Scripture simply begins, "In the beginning God created the heavens and the earth" (Gen. 1:1).

In contrast, God's Word pulls no punches when it comments on those who deny the existence and reality of God: "The fool has said in his heart, 'There is no God.' They are corrupt, they have committed abominable deeds; there is no one who does good" (Ps. 14:1; see also 10:4; 53:1).

Whether you examine the macro-world of space or the human body with its intricate details, logic demands that we conclude the existence of God. When there is design, there must be a designer. For every effect, surely there is a cause. Life demands a life-giver. Centuries ago Sir Isaac Newton wrote, "In the absence of other proofs, the thumb alone would convince me of God's existence."

God's existence becomes the only reasonable conclusion for a thinking person with an open mind. To say there is no God admits that the world came into existence by random chance, better described as an accident.

With accident logic, you could believe that a Pulitzer Prize-winning novel originated by throwing a type tray into the air and having it land in the exact words of the book. Or that a 747 jet came into being when a tornado went through a junkyard. These illustrations seem absurd, but they are less so than questioning the existence of God. Blind absurdity leads to atheism. Reasonable faith concludes that God exists.

The position of an atheist results in dramatic, even traumatic, conclusions about life. If you know someone who entertains the thought, here are several questions with which you can test that person's certainty:

1. Have you traveled everywhere in the universe and beyond to verify there is no God?
2. If God were invisible and you could not see Him, does that deny His reality?
3. Do you know enough about God to recognize Him if you did see Him?
4. Have you read all that there is to read about God, including the Bible, to make sure your conclusions come from a complete set of facts?

Is God Knowable?

Religious people usually waffle on this one. Take the Athenians in Paul's day, for example. They admitted to many gods, including the unknown god.

> *And Paul stood in the midst of the Areopagus and said,*
> *"Men of Athens, I observe that you are very religious in all*
> *respects. For while I was passing through and examining*
> *the objects of your worship, I also found an altar with this*
> *inscription, 'TO AN UNKNOWN GOD.' What therefore*
> *you worship in ignorance, this I proclaim to you. The God*
> *who made the world and all things in it, since He is Lord*
> *of heaven and earth, does not dwell in temples made with*
> *hands; neither is He served by human hands, as though He*
> *needed anything, since He Himself gives to all life and*
> *breath and all things; and He made from one, every nation*
> *of mankind to live on all the face of the earth, having*
> *determined their appointed times, and the boundaries of*
> *their habitation, that they should seek God, if perhaps they*
> *might grope for Him and find Him, though He is not far*
> *from each one of us; for in Him we live and move and*
> *exist, as even some of your own poets have said, 'For we*
> *also are His offspring.'*
>
> *"Being then the offspring of God, we ought not to think*
> *that the Divine Nature is like gold or silver or stone, an*
> *image formed by the art and thought of man. Therefore*
> *having overlooked the times of ignorance, God is now de-*
> *claring to men that all everywhere should repent, because*
> *He has fixed a day in which He will judge the world in*
> *righteousness through a Man whom He has appointed,*
> *having furnished proof to all men by raising Him from the*
> *dead" (Acts 17:22-31).*

God surrounds us on all sides with knowledge about Himself. When we look up at the heavens, they declare God's
glory (Ps. 19:1). A knowledge of God resides intuitively evi-
dent within mankind (Rom. 1:19). Scripture everywhere tells
of God from Genesis 1:1 to Revelation 22:21. The person of
Jesus Christ explained God the Father (John 1:18). God cer-

tainly does not engage in a game of hide-and-seek, but rather has gone out of His way to be obvious.

What's more, God made known His salvation (Ps. 16:11; 98:2) through Jesus Christ.

All things have been handed over to Me by My Father; and no one knows the Son, except the Father; nor does anyone know the Father, except the Son, and anyone to whom the Son wills to reveal Him (Matt. 11:27).

However, if we limit our search for God through human resources alone, the data will be misinterpreted and mankind will bypass the obvious.

For since in the wisdom of God the world through its wisdom did not come to know God, God was well-pleased through the foolishness of the message preached to save those who believe (1 Cor. 1:21).

Knowing about God

For those who admit the existence of God and that God can be known, they experience a seeking process during which they crave to know about God, to know who He is, how He operates, and where He can be found.

Some, like Pharaoh, admit they do not know God (Ex. 5:2), while others, like Nebuchadnezzar, know God in interesting ways (Dan. 4:34-37). But knowing factually is not enough. Listen to Paul's commentary on a whole category of God knowers:

For even though they knew God, they did not honor Him as God, or give thanks; but they became futile in their speculations, and their foolish heart was darkened (Rom. 1:21).

They knew facts about God but their knowledge never progressed to knowing God personally.

On the other hand, many seek God the best way and in the most sincere manner possible. Take Cornelius, for example. Even though he came from a Gentile background, he was nevertheless a devout man, one who feared God, gave many alms, and prayed continually (Acts 10:2). Cornelius wanted more than facts or philosophical speculations; he desired to go beyond the mere intellectual side of knowing God to the spiritual. The same proved true of Lydia who as a worshiper of God had not yet moved from the knowledge of God to a relationship with Him (16:12-15).

Let me illustrate from the lives of two men who greatly differ in religious backgrounds. Listen to Gandhi who admitted to being a devout admirer of Jesus Christ but rejected a personal relationship with Him:

The convention lasted for three days. I could understand and appreciate devoutness of those who attended it. But I saw no reason for changing my belief—my religion. It was impossible for me to believe that I could go to heaven or attain salvation only by becoming a Christian. When I frankly said so to some of the good Christian friends, they were shocked. But there was no help for it.

My difficulties lay deeper. It was more than I could believe that Jesus was the only incarnate son of God, and that only he who believed in Him would have everlasting life. If God could have sons, all of us were His sons. If Jesus was like God, or God Himself, then all men were like God and could be God Himself. My reason was not ready to believe literally that Jesus by His death and by His blood redeemed the sins of the world. Again, according to Christianity only human beings had souls, and not other living beings, for whom death meant complete extinction; while I held a contrary belief. I could accept Jesus as a martyr, an embodiment of sacrifice, and a divine teacher, but not as the most perfect man ever born. His death on the Cross was a great example to the world, but that there was anything like a mysterious or miraculous virtue in it my heart could not accept. The pious lives of Christians did not give me anything that the lives of men of other faiths had failed to give. I had seen in other lives just the same reformation that I had heard among Christians. Philosophically there was nothing extraordinary in Christian principles. From the point of view of sacrifice, it seemed to me that the Hindus greatly surpasses the Christians. It was impossible for me to regard Christianity as a perfect religion or the greatest of all religions.

I shared this mental churning with my Christian friends whenever there was an opportunity, but their answers could not satisfy me.[3]   ,

Compare that with Rabbi Max Wertheimer who knew about God factually but one day discovered that this knowledge alone could not provide eternal life:

Born in Germany of devout Jewish parents, my first fifteen years were saturated with training in Orthodox Judaism. Then I began my studies toward a career and was apprenticed to a manufacturer doing office work. Although I continued to read the prayers and attend synagogue, my worldly associates led me into sinful pleasures, and I drifted from the faith of my fathers.

My parents sent me to America to pursue a classical education. . . . Four years after completing my undergraduate work I received my Master's Degree.

Having become proficient in the translation of Hebrew into the vernacular and with a complete knowledge of Jewish history, I was ordained and inducted into rabbinical office. I served ten years in my first charge, receiving many tokens of affection from my flock. I contributed much to their knowledge of the social, industrial, and economic problems of the day. I spoke of monotheism, ethical culture, and the moral systems of the Jews. On Sabbath mornings I gave addresses on the Pentateuch, and on Sundays I taught from eight in the morning to five in the evening with only an hour's break for dinner.

Suddenly, there came a change. My wife became seriously ill and soon died, leaving me a distraught widower with two small children. I could not sleep. I walked the streets striving to find something that would make me forget the void in my life. My dreams were shattered. Where was comfort to be found? I called on the God of my fathers, but the heavens seemed as brass. How could I speak words of comfort to others when my own sorrow had brought me to despair? I delved into Spiritism, Theosophy, and Christian Science, only to find them futile and hopeless.

Again I studied Judaism, but it answered no questions; it satisfied no craving in my heart. Then I began to read the New Testament, comparing it with the Old. As I pondered over and meditated on many passages, one in particular made a definite impression, "... my righteous servant," found in the eleventh verse [Isa. 53;11]. This was the only mention of that phrase I could find in either Testament. We have, "David, my servant," "Isaiah, my servant," "Daniel, my servant," but here it is, "My righteous servant."

I could hold out in unbelief no longer. I was convinced of the truth of God as it is in Christ Jesus. I cried, "Lord, I believe that Thou as Jehovah Yesous hast made the atonement for me. I believe that Jehovah Yesous died for me! From henceforth I will publicly confess Yeshua as my Savior and Lord!" Thus, after months of searching, I was convinced that Jesus was the righteous servant of Jehovah, Jehovah-tsidkenu, "The Lord our righteousness."[4]

Knowing God Personally

To the Jews, like Rabbi Wertheimer, who knew all about God historically, Jesus came so that they could know God personally. John writes in his Gospel, "He was in the world, and the world was made through Him, and the world did not know Him. . . . And this is eternal life, that they may know Thee, the only true God, and Jesus Christ whom Thou hast sent" (John 1:10; 17:3).

Paul frequently spoke about people who knew facts about God but had not entered into a relational knowledge of God: "However at that time, when you did not know God, you were slaves to those which by nature are no gods" (Gal. 4:8; see also 1 Thes. 4:5; 2 Thes. 1:8).

Now look at Galatians 4:9: "But now that you have come to know God, or rather to be known by God. . . ." Paul does not question the Galatians' factual knowledge nor God's omniscience, but rather contrasts the time when a personal relationship did not exist with the time when they put their faith in Christ (2:15-16) and entered into a personal relationship. They knew and were known.

John presents this truth very directly: "And we know that the Son of God has come, and has given us understanding, in order that we might know Him who is true, and we are in Him who is true, in His Son Jesus Christ. This is the true God and eternal life" (1 John 5:20).

That's exactly what the Prophet Hosea meant when he wrote, "For I delight in loyalty rather than sacrifice, and in the knowledge of God rather than burnt offerings" (Hosea 6:6).

At this point, let me issue a warning: Always proceed from the step of factual knowledge to the step of relationship on God's terms alone. There have been those who foolishly tried their own way (with great sincerity), but in the end God did not acknowledge their acquaintance. The issue is not only "Do I know God?" but also "Does God know me?"

Not everyone who says to Me, "Lord, Lord," will enter the kingdom of heaven; but he who does the will of My Father who is in heaven. Many will say to Me on that day, "Lord, Lord, did we not prophesy in Your name, and in Your name cast out demons, and in Your name perform many miracles?" And then I will declare to them, "I never knew you; depart from Me, you who practice lawlessness" (Matt. 7:21-23).

Paul tells the Cretians, "They profess to know God, but by their deeds they deny Him, being detestable and disobedient, and worthless for any good deed" (Titus 1:16).

Be confident, God knows. He knows the ones who are righteously related to Him in Jesus Christ. "For the Lord knows the way of the righteous, but the way of the wicked will perish" (Ps. 1:6).

God makes the difference. Myra Brooks Welch expresses this grand truth beautifully in "The Touch of the Master's Hand."

Twas battered and scarred, and the auctioneer
Thought it scarcely worth his while
To waste much time on the old violin,
But held it up with a smile.
"What am I bidden, good folks," he cried,
"Who will start bidding for me?
A dollar, a dollar"—then, "Two!" "Only two?
Two dollars, and who'll make it three?
Three dollars, once; three dollars, twice;
Going for three—" But no,
From the room, far back, a gray-haired man
Came forward and picked up the bow;
Then, wiping the dust from the old violin,
And tightening the loose strings,
He played a melody pure and sweet
As sweet as a caroling angel sings.

The music ceased, and the auctioneer,
With a voice that was quiet and low,
Said, "What am I bidden for the old violin?"

And he held it up with the bow.
"A thousand dollars, and who'll make it two?
Two thousand! And who'll make it three?
Three thousand, once; three thousand, twice;
And going, and gone!" said he.
The people cheered, but some of them cried,
"We do not quite understand
What changed its worth?" Swift came the reply:
"The touch of the master's hand."

And many a man with life out of tune,
And battered and scarred with sin,
Is auctioned cheap to the thoughtless crowd,
Much like the old violin.
A "mess of pottage," a glass of wine;
A game—and he travels on.
He's "going" once, and "going" twice,
He's "going" and "almost gone."
But the Master comes, and the foolish crowd
Never can quite understand
The worth of a soul, and the change that's wrought
By the touch of the Master's hand.[5]

Knowing God Intimately

In the *New King James Version,* Genesis 4:1 reads: "Now Adam *knew* Eve his wife, and she conceived." Adam did not only know his wife factually or just personally but also in the most intimate sense. As they knew intimacy at its deepest level maritally, we can know God in the richest way spiritually. That should be our desire, like the psalmist who pleaded, "Search me, O God, and know my heart; try me and know my anxious thoughts" (Ps. 139:23).

For humans to know and understand God unquestionably causes God's delight (see also 1 Cor. 1:31; 2 Cor. 10:17):

Thus says the Lord, "Let not a wise man boast of his

wisdom, and let not the mighty man boast of his might, let not the rich man boast of his riches; but let him who boasts boast of this, that he understands and knows Me, that I am the Lord who exercises loving-kindness, justice, and righteousness on earth; for I delight in these things," declares the Lord (Jer. 9:23-24).

The New Testament uses *Abba* only three times in reference to God (Mark 14:36; Rom. 8:15; Gal. 4:6). That's the most tender word of endearment possible and expresses an element of our childlike delight in the Father. These three uses correspond in emphasis to the three Hebrew words translated "delight" in the Old Testament which speak of our relationship with God. First, there is the personal delight in God spoken of in Psalm 37:4:

Delight yourself in the Lord; and He will give you the desires of your heart.

It expresses a delicate or close relational delight or intimacy (see also Isa. 58:2). It corresponds to the Abba of Galatians 4:6:

And because you are sons, God has sent forth the Spirit of His Son into our hearts, crying, "Abba! Father!"

Next, our delight should be in God's Word, illustrated in Psalm 1:2:

But his delight is in the law of the Lord, and in His law he meditates day and night.

This delight of our will focuses on what God has said to us. Note its counterpart in Romans 8:15:

For you have not received a spirit of slavery leading to fear again, but you have received a spirit of adoption as sons by which we cry out, "Abba! Father!"

The third delight of intimacy comes in doing God's will, spoken of in Psalm 40:8:

I delight to do Thy will, O my God; Thy law is within my heart.

This emotional expression has its parallel in Christ's Gethsemane prayer recorded in Mark 14:36:

And he was saying, "Abba! Father! All things are possible for Thee; remove this cup from Me; yet not what I will, but what Thou wilt."

Ibrahim's true story relates the depth of intimacy and commitment which a Christian can have, by God's grace, with our Heavenly Father. This 22-year-old former Muslim from the Central African Republic had to choose his own punishment for accepting Christ. Lose his mind. Be inflicted with an incurable sickness. Or death.

After hearing about Ibrahim putting his faith in the Lord Jesus Christ, the Islamic council of his town called a meeting. There they sought Allah's forgiveness for Ibrahim's departure, while accusing him of leading three other Muslims to hell. Finally they gave him his choice from any of the three punishments because of his "apostasy." By God's protective hand, he was able to escape from his religious torture; but either way Ibrahim knew an Abba intimacy with God, for he delighted in God personally, in God's Word, and in God's will. Even if it would have cost him his life.

Significant Questions
An old preacher and a professional actor both attended a social gathering to honor the actor. The actor received many

requests to recite portions of well-known works. The preacher requested Psalm 23.

The actor agreed only if the preacher would recite the piece too. After the actor concluded, the crowd clapped for his professional delivery and flawless expression. Then came the preacher's turn. He read haltingly with a raspy voice, but when he finished the audience wept.

Someone leaned over and asked the actor, "What caused the difference?" He candidly admitted, "I know the psalm but he knows the Shepherd."

Do you know about the Shepherd? Or do you know Him personally? Perhaps intimately? Do you live life *coram deo,* consciously in the presence of God?

It all begins with a right relationship. Jesus extends this invitation to all: "Come to Me, all who are weary and heavy-laden, and I will give you rest. Take My yoke upon you, and learn from Me, for I am gentle and humble in heart; and you shall find rest for your souls. For My yoke is easy, and My load is light" (Matt. 11:28-30).

Think about your personal relationship with God in terms of a prisoner being set free (Col. 1:13-14). John Mohr paints the picture with these striking words.

All are born prisoners of war.
Victims, yet fully responsible.
Then, the news of liberation.
Stories of prisoners escaping to freedom.
Some believe.
Some refuse.
And then, the rumor:
"The prison doors have been unlocked."
Some believe—and escape.
Some believe, but for fear remain.
I remained.
One day a cellmate took courage,
Tried the door, and found it open.

He called back, "It's true . . . there is freedom . . . come
and see!"
Now, I knew.
Still I refused.
The price paid for truth refused
Is always too great to bear.
Until one day, in misery and desperation,
I threw myself against the cell door . . .
Eyes blind with tears
Could scarcely believe.
I lay in brokenness
Outside the prison walls.
The sun shone warm on my shivering soul.
The air, buoyant with peace.
I stood.
I inhaled freedom,
And for the very first time,
Filled my lungs without a ragged breath. [6]

Now, as a liberated child of the Heavenly Father, you can
desire with Paul, "That I may know Him, and the power of
His resurrection and the fellowship of His sufferings, being
conformed to His death; in order that I may attain to the
resurrection from the dead" (Phil. 3:10-11).

Also, as one who has been forgiven your sins and spared
from their penalty by God's grace in Jesus Christ, you can
exclaim:

Oh, the depth of the riches both of the wisdom and knowl-
edge of God! How unsearchable are His judgments and
unfathomable His ways! For who has known the mind of
the Lord, or who became His counselor? Or who has first
given to Him that it might be paid back again? For from
Him and through Him and to Him are all things. To Him
be the glory forever. Amen (Rom. 11:33-36).

Teach me, O Lord, the way of Thy statutes,
And I shall observe it to the end.
Give me understanding, that I may observe Thy law,
And keep it with all my heart.
Make me walk in the path of Thy commandments,
For I delight in it.
Psalm 119:33-35

2
LISTENING TO GOD

A well-known Christian author recently wrote, "Anyone who comes to the Bible with a primary purpose of gaining knowledge about theology misses its message. We must come with the purpose of understanding ourselves better so we can know God better."[1]

At first glance that sounds OK. We all agree that studying Scripture should not stop with information but continue on to personal transformation. Now think a little longer. Do we understand God better by first understanding ourselves? After all, who created whom?

God, through the Prophet Isaiah, declared, "My thoughts are not your thoughts, neither are your ways My ways. . . . For as the heavens are higher than the earth, so are My ways higher than your ways, and My thoughts than your thoughts" (Isa. 55:8-9). Since His ways and thoughts differ radically from ours, we should start with Him—not ourselves—if we're to know and be what He wants us to be. To know God, we must start with Scripture for that is where He gives the most intimate glimpses of Himself and His design for spiritual well-being.

Cultivating Intimacy

One of the most effective ways to cultivate a deeper relationship with God is talking to Him (prayer). Learn to speak freely with God about your concerns for others, your circumstances, your sin (confession), and your need for Him. Let your desire to be intimate with Him show by how you communicate with Him. Numerous other activities help cultivate a deeper relationship with God: worshiping in spirit and in truth, being filled with God's Spirit, praising God with thanksgiving, giving sacrificially to build Christ's church, walking in God's will, and framing your life with a desire to glorify Him in all things.

But your pursuit of intimacy can be detoured, ineffective, or even wasteful if you have not entered at the right gateway. All those wonderful practices presuppose that you know what God desires from His children and that you are acting in accord with His specific instructions in the Bible.

The key to a great relationship with your spouse and children is good communication—particularly listening. That is also true of our relationship with God. Through Scripture, we can listen to and know the mind of God (Ps. 19:7-11; 1 Cor. 2:6-16). By it we entered God's family (1 Peter 1:23), and by it we can grow to spiritual maturity (Ps. 119; 1 Thes. 2:13).

Good communication heightens with intimacy. God's Word reveals all that we need to know about Him, His plan, and our relationship with Him. The Bible is God's way of talking to us. Scripture is like a photo album of other family members, a diary of past events, a calendar of future plans, a letter from home, a revealing portrait of God, and descriptions of acceptable family behavior.

Only in Scripture do we get intimate glances into the history of God's involvement with this world (Genesis to Esther). Or glimpses into the diaries of men like Job, the psalmists, or Solomon. Proverbs and Ecclesiastes contain the treasures of God's wisdom. In the prophets, we learn of God's faithfulness to reward obedience and punish sin. The New Testament introduces us to God's Son in the Gospels, His church in Acts and the Epistles, and earth's ultimate destiny in Revelation.

Without Scripture, we would know relatively little about Him. Our level of intimacy would be extremely limited. To be specific, our praise would be incomplete (Ps. 119:164), our lives lacking the Spirit's power (Eph. 5:18-21; Col. 3:16-17), our prayers aimless (1 John 5:14-15), our love for God empty since it is manifested by obeying Scripture (John 14:15; 2 John 6), our fellowship with God shallow (1 John 1:3), and worship of Him misdirected since it is based on walking in the light of His Word (John 4:24).

Mankind's original intimacy with God collapsed because Adam and Eve listened to another's word and disobeyed God's Word (Gen. 3:1-19). Spiritual intimacy returns only when our attitudes and actions are based on Scripture.

The Bible clearly illustrates the connection between knowing God and knowing Scripture. God looks with favor on humble individuals who tremble at His Word (Isa. 66:2, 5). Just like God spoke to Moses as a friend (Ex. 33:11), so God will speak to Christians through His Word as a special friend. Here is an illustrious listing of individuals who counted on the certainty of these truths:

Daniel (Dan. 9:1-23); Jeremiah (Jer. 15:16); Jesus (Matt. 4:4); Job (Job 23:12); Joshua (Josh. 1:8-9); Josiah (2 Kings 23:3); Paul (2 Tim. 3:16-17); and Solomon (Ecc. 12:13-14).

How well we would do to stand in their company by trembling at the Lord's Word.

Opening the Gate
The thought of personal Bible study intimidates many Christians. It seems so formidable when you have little or no

formal training. Yet Psalm 119 beckons every true worshiper to feed on the spiritual nourishment provided by the Holy Scriptures, and thereby grow in spiritual intimacy with God.

Whether you are a pastor with several theological degrees or a new babe in Christ, this series of simple steps for fruitful Bible study will successfully lead you into the Word of God. You can come away with the deep satisfaction of knowing that the living God has spoken to you through His Word, that you understand the message, and that you have drawn closer to your Heavenly Father's side.

Step 1—Affirmation: Prayerfully acknowledge before God that you recognize His book, the Bible, to be the only written expression of His will given to mankind. Thus it is the absolute authority for both your beliefs and behavior (Matt. 5:18; 24:35; 2 Tim. 3:16).

Step 2—Preparation: Prayerfully ask God to open your eyes (Ps. 119:18), teach you His statutes (v. 12), and establish your ways by His Word (v. 5).

Step 3—Observation: Carefully read your Bible to discover what it says. Study it systematically. Good Christian books and magazines that supplement your Bible reading are also helpful, but there is no substitute for reading Scripture itself.

Step 4—Investigation: Consult Bible commentaries, dictionaries, encyclopedias, and atlases to see what other godly people have observed.

Step 5—Interpretation: Analyze all those observations to discover what God meant by what He said. Use the normal rules for literary interpretation—as you would for any other piece of literature—and seek the Spirit's illuminating help (Ps. 119:102; 1 John 2:27).

Step 6—Correlation: Use the cross-references in your Bible or a work like *The Treasury of Scripture Knowledge*[2] to discover the totality of what God has said about a particular theme or idea that you're interested in. You will understand the whole only when you've taken time to assemble all the parts.

Step 7—Appropriation: Your Bible study is never complete

until you apply what you have learned to your life. Transfer the fruit of your labors from the head and heart to the hands and feet. James 4:17 (NIV) says, "Anyone, then, who knows the good he ought to do and doesn't do it, sins."

Step 8—Proclamation: Ask God to bring someone into your life on a daily basis with whom you can share your exciting discoveries in God's Word. Don't be silent about the most precious book ever written—someone's life might depend on it.[3]

Take heed to our Lord's conversation with Mary and Martha (Luke 10:38-42). It's a great statement on the number-one priority of the Word. Jesus commended Mary for "listening to the Lord's Word" (v. 39), but scolded Martha for putting her service above her God (vv. 41-42).

Fueling God's Spirit

The Bible promises tremendous spiritual blessing to those who devote their time to it.

This book of the law shall not depart from your mouth, but you shall meditate on it day and night, so that you may be careful to do according to all that is written in it; for then you will make your way prosperous, and then you will have success (Josh. 1:8).

But his delight is in the law of the Lord, and in His law he meditates day and night. And he will be like a tree firmly planted by streams of water (Ps. 1:2-3).

Blessed is he who reads and those who hear the words of the prophecy, and heed the things which are written in it; for the time is near (Rev. 1:3).

But so few people seem to experience what God wants to deliver. Why?

Look carefully at these next two passages. What feature do they share in common? What features distinguish them?

Let the word of Christ richly dwell within you, with all wisdom teaching and admonishing one another with psalms and hymns and spiritual songs, singing with thankfulness in your hearts to God. And whatever you do in word or deed, do all in the name of the Lord Jesus, giving thanks through Him to God the Father (Col. 3:16-17).

And do not get drunk with wine, for that is dissipation, but be filled with the Spirit, speaking to one another in psalms and hymns and spiritual songs, singing and making melody with your heart to the Lord; always giving thanks for all things in the name of our Lord Jesus Christ to God, even the Father; and be subject to one another in the fear of Christ (Eph. 5:18-21).

The results are almost identical, but the means seem to be different. Let me suggest that both means—the Holy Spirit and the Bible—blend together in the total process. Think about it! As believers, we all have the Holy Spirit, but we do not have equal experiences with the Word. I'm suggesting that it is the combination of Scripture along with the Holy Spirit that produces vitality in the believer's life.

Let me illustrate by comparing this spiritual process to starting a car. God's Spirit is the engine, your will serves as the ignition key, and God's Word acts as fuel. If you have an engine without fuel, you can turn the ignition key all you want but the car will not start. Without the Word, the power of the Holy Spirit will go unignited.

You can have the best of engines and a tank full of the best fuel, but until the ignition is turned there will be no energy. So the Holy Spirit and the Word without the cooperation of the human will are essentially dormant.

However, with a perfect engine, a tank of high-octane fuel, and timely ignition, you have all the power needed to drive. Likewise, with the Holy Spirit, rich portions of the Word, and your will desiring God's will, you have all of the spiritual energy and blessing you could ever want. All three elements need to be in sync before anything significant happens.

God's Word at Work

You might be wondering, "If all three elements are true in my life, what actual results can I expect?" Note Paul's broad answer—the Word performs spiritual work: "And for this reason we also constantly thank God that when you received from us the word of God's message, you accepted it not as the word of men, but for what it really is, the word of God, which also performs its work in you who believe" (1 Thes. 2:13).

Now carefully consider some of the specifics of how it:

1. SAVES US
1 Peter 1:23—"For you have been born again not of seed which is perishable but imperishable, that is, through the living and abiding word of God."

2. TEACHES US
2 Timothy 3:16—"All Scripture is inspired by God and profitable for teaching . . ."

3. REBUKES US
2 Timothy 3:16—"for reproof . . ."

4. CORRECTS US
2 Timothy 3:16-17—"for correction . . . "

5. DISCIPLES US
2 Timothy 3:16-17—"for training in righteousness . . ."

6. EQUIPS US
2 Timothy 3:17—"that the man of God may be adequate, equipped for every good work."

7. GUIDES US

Psalm 119:105 — "Thy word is a lamp to my feet, and a light to my path."

8. COUNSELS US

Psalm 119:24 — "Thy testimonies also are my delight; they are my counselors."

9. REVIVES US

Psalm 119:154 — "Plead my cause and redeem me; revive me according to Thy word."

10. RESTORES OUR SOUL

Psalm 19:7 — "The law of the Lord is perfect, restoring the soul; the testimony of the Lord is sure, making wise the simple."

11. WARNS US/REWARDS US

Psalm 19:11 — "Moreover, by them Thy servant is warned; in keeping them there is great reward."

12. NOURISHES US

1 Peter 2:2 — "Like newborn babes, long for the pure milk of the word, that by it you may grow in respect to salvation."

13. JUDGES US

Hebrews 4:12 — "For the word of God is living and active and sharper than any two-edged sword, and piercing as far as the division of soul and spirit, of both joints and marrow, and able to judge the thoughts and intentions of the heart."

14. SANCTIFIES US

John 17:17 — "Sanctify them in the truth; Thy word is truth."

15. FREES US

John 8:31-32 — "Jesus therefore was saying to those Jews who had believed Him, 'If you abide in My word, then you are truly disciples of Mine; and you shall know the truth, and the truth shall make you free.' "

16. ENRICHES US

Colossians 3:16 — "Let the word of Christ richly dwell within you, with all wisdom teaching and admonishing one another with psalms and hymns and spiritual songs, singing with thankfulness in your hearts to God."

17. PROTECTS US

Psalm 119:11 — "Thy word I have treasured in my heart, that I may not sin against Thee."

18. STRENGTHENS US

Psalm 119:28 — "My soul weeps because of grief; strengthen me according to Thy word."

19. MAKES US WISE

Psalm 119:97-100 — "O how I love Thy law! It is my meditation all the day. Thy commandments make me wiser than my enemies, for they are ever mine. I have more insight than all my teachers, for Thy testimonies are my meditation. I understand more than the aged, because I have observed Thy precepts."

20. REJOICES OUR HEART

Psalm 19:8 — "The precepts of the Lord are right, rejoicing the heart; the commandment of the Lord is pure, enlightening the eyes."

The Normal Christian Life

Let me introduce you to some people in Scripture who exemplified a key element in having a right relationship to God's

Word. If you will incorporate each of these examples into your experience, you can lead the normal Christian life.

First, *Job* hungered for and craved God's Word. He prioritized spiritual nourishment higher than the physical. "I have not departed from the command of His lips; I have treasured the words of His mouth more than my necessary food" (Job 23:12).

Second, *Caleb* fully obeyed God's Word. He understood the Word as orders from above with the obligation to follow in every detail. "But My servant Caleb, because he has had a different spirit and has followed Me fully, I will bring into the land which he entered, and his descendants shall take possession of it" (Num. 14:24).

Third, the *post-Captivity Jews* honored God's Word. When the Word was opened, it was like God entered their presence. They responded with appropriate respect. "And Ezra opened the book in the sight of all the people for he was standing above all the people; and when he opened it, all the people stood up. Then Ezra blessed the Lord the great God. And all the people answered, 'Amen, Amen!' while lifting up their hands; then they bowed low and worshiped the Lord with their faces to the ground" (Neh. 8:5-6).

Fourth, *Ezra* studied God's Word. He viewed Scripture not as a shallow stream to wade in but rather a deep river in which to swim. "For Ezra had set his heart to study the law of the Lord, and to practice it, and to teach His statutes and ordinances in Israel" (Ezra 7:10).

Fifth, *Apollos* understood God's Word. Accuracy became his hallmark. "Now a certain Jew named Apollos, an Alexandrian by birth, an eloquent man, came to Ephesus; and he was mighty in the Scriptures. This man had been instructed in the way of the Lord; and being fervent in spirit, he was speaking and teaching accurately the things concerning Jesus, being acquainted only with the baptism of John" (Acts 18:24-25).

Sixth, *Paul* discipled faithful and able men in the Scriptures. He realized the responsibility to hand the Word on to coming generations. "And the things which you have heard from me in the presence of many witnesses, these entrust to faithful men who will be able to teach others also" (2 Tim. 2:2).

A Daily Pursuit

Intimacy with God is not limited to ancient history. God's Word remains fresh and powerful (Ps. 119:89-90; Isa. 55:11). However, according to a recent Gallup poll, only a small percentage of American Christians spend time daily in God's Word. If your Bible wrote a diary about its use, how would it read? Here is an imaginary report of one such Bible:

Jan. 15 — Been resting for a week. A few nights after the first of the year my owner opened me, but no more. Another New Year's resolution gone awry.

Feb. 3 — Owner picked me up and rushed off to Sunday School.

Feb. 23 — Cleaning day. Was dusted and put back in my place.

April 2 — Busy day. Owner had to present the lesson at a church society meeting. Quickly looked up a lot of references.

May 5 — In Grandma's lap again, a comfortable place.

May 9 — She let a tear fall on John 14:1-3.

May 10 — Grandma's gone. Back in my old place.

May 20 — Baby born. They wrote his name on one of my pages.

July 1 — Packed in a suitcase — off for a vacation.

July 20 — Still in the suitcase. Almost everything else taken out.

July 25 — Home again. Quite a journey, though I don't see why I went.

Aug. 16 — Cleaned again and put in a prominent place. The minister is to be here for dinner.

Aug. 20 — Owner wrote Grandma's death in my family record. He left his extra pair of glasses between my pages.

Dec. 31 — Owner just found his glasses. Wonder if he will make any resolutions about me for the New Year.

If you wouldn't want anyone to read your Bible's diary, let

me suggest two helps that will encourage you to have a daily visit with God in His Word. *The Daily Walk* (from Walk Thru the Bible Ministries) and *The One Year Bible* (Tyndale) have proved invaluable to me; I highly recommend them to you as well. Then develop the daily habit of reading and studying not just for information but for intimacy.

The framed words of this wonderful charter hang on the wall at the entrance to my study. They always remind me that in the Bible, I have all of God's provision for intimacy with Him:

This book contains: the mind of God, the state of man, the way of salvation, the doom of sinners, and the happiness of believers.

Its doctrine is holy, its precepts are binding, its histories are true, and its decisions are immutable.

Read it to be wise, believe it to be safe, and practice it to be holy.

It contains light to direct you, food to support you, and comfort to cheer you.

It is the traveler's map, the pilgrim's staff, the pilot's compass, the soldier's sword, and the Christian's charter.

Here heaven is opened, and the gates of hell disclosed.

Christ is its grand subject, our good its design, and the glory of God its end.

It should fill the memory, rule the heart, and guide the feet.

Read it slowly, frequently, and prayerfully.

It is a mine of wealth, health to the soul, and a river of pleasure.

It is given to you here in this life, will be opened at the Judgment, and is established forever.

It involves the highest responsibility, will reward the greatest labor, and condemns all who trifle with its contents.

Intimacy with God is not reserved for a select group of

initiates but is within the grasp of every believer. There's no magic formula. In fact, there are no shortcuts, only one, well-marked path—the Word of God. Read it. Study it. Make its truths yours. It is the only gateway to your growing intimacy with God.

Let the words of my mouth and the meditation
of my heart be acceptable in Thy sight,
O Lord, my rock and my redeemer.
Psalm 19:14

3
THINKING LIKE GOD

Jim Downing tells this insightful story.

An Oriental fable tells of three horsemen who were travel-
ing through the desert at night. Unexpectedly they were
confronted by a mysterious person. The stranger told them
that they would soon cross the dry bed of a stream.

"When you arrive there," he declared, "get off your hors-
es and fill your pockets and saddle bags from the river bed.
At sunrise examine the stones you have picked up. You will
be both glad and sorry."

As the man predicted, the travelers came to a dry stream
bed. In the spirit of adventure they put a few of the many
stones they found scattered into their pockets. At sunrise the
next day they examined the pebbles they had picked up. To
their great astonishment they found the stones had been
transformed into diamonds, rubies, emeralds, and other
precious stones.

*Recalling the statement of the stranger in the desert, they
understood what he meant — they were glad for the pebbles
they had picked up but sorry they hadn't taken more.* [1]

With all of God's infallible wisdom available in unlimited
quantities we, like the horsemen, wish in hindsight that we
had picked up more. This sounds very much like Solomon's
woes in Ecclesiastes, where he wrote, "And I set my mind to
seek and explore by wisdom concerning all that has been
done under heaven. It is a grievous task which God has given
to the sons of men to be afflicted with. . . . And I set my mind
to know wisdom and to know madness and folly; I realized
that this also is striving after wind. Because in much wisdom
there is much grief, and increasing knowledge results in increasing pain" (Ecc. 1:13, 17-18).

Even though Solomon had God's wisdom abundantly available (1 Kings 3:12), he chose to think like man, not God.

Control Center

The brain is key to human existence. It weighs only three
pounds but determines what the rest of our much heavier
body does. It consumes 25 percent of our blood's oxygen
supply, handles 10,000 thoughts daily, regulates over 103,000
heartbeats every 24 hours, controls over 600 muscles, and
coordinates over 23,000 breaths a day.

Not only does the brain control our physical life but also
our emotions, our will, our thinking, and our spiritual life.
What we do with our mind determines what we do with our
life.

This central truth did not escape the notice of an ancient
writer of Scripture, who commented, "For as he thinks within himself, so he is" (Prov. 23:7). Another proverb says:

Sow a thought, reap an act.
Sow an act, reap a habit.
Sow a habit, reap a character.

Christianity claims to be and certainly is a religion of the mind. Listen to Paul:

For those who are according to the flesh set their minds on the things of the flesh, but those who are according to the Spirit, the things of the Spirit. For the mind set on the flesh is hostile toward God, for it does not subject itself to the law of God, for it is not even able to do so; and those who are in the flesh cannot please God (Rom. 8:5-7).

Jesus admonished Christians to love God with all of their mind (Matt. 22:37). How we think and who we think like determines the course of our life. The brain becomes central to thinking like God and then loving God.

The Renewed Mind
When you entered into a personal relationship with Jesus Christ, you became a new creation (2 Cor. 5:17) who now sings a new song (Ps. 98:1). But that does not mean that everything becomes new in the sense of perfection. Your mind acquired a new way to think and a new capacity to clean up your old ways of thinking. God is in the business of mind renewal.

And do not be conformed to this world, but be transformed by the renewing of your mind, that you may prove what the will of God is, that which is good and acceptable and perfect (Rom. 12:2).

And that you be renewed in the spirit of your mind (Eph. 4:23).

And have put on the new self who is being renewed to a true knowledge according to the image of the One who created him (Col. 3:10).

Then the Bible tells us to "set our minds on the things

above, not on the things that are on earth" (Col. 3:2). Paul put this concept in military terms: "We are destroying speculations and every lofty thing raised up against the knowledge of God, and we are taking every thought captive to the obedience of Christ" (2 Cor. 10:5).

How do we do this? Scripture is the mind of God. Not all of His mind, to be sure; but all that God cared to give us. To think like God, we must think like Scripture. That's why Paul encouraged the Colossians to let the word of Christ richly dwell within them (Col. 3:16).

Henry Blamires, an Englishman with extraordinary understanding about thinking Christianly, puts this quite well:

To think Christianly is to think in terms of Revelation. For the secularist, God and theology are the playthings of the mind. For the Christian, God is real, and Christian theology describes His truth revealed to us. For the secular mind, religion is essentially a matter of theory: for the Christian mind, Christianity is a matter of acts and facts. The acts and facts which are the basis of our faith are recorded in the Bible.[2]

Meditation

To hear something once for most of us is not enough. To briefly ponder something profound for most of us does not allow enough time to grasp and fully understand its significance. This proves to be most true with God's mind in Scripture.

The idea of meditating sometimes lends itself to misunderstanding, so let me illustrate its meaning. Meditation involves prolonged thought or pondering. Our American figure of speech is "to chew" on a thought. Some have likened it to the rumination process of the cow's double stomach digestive system.

For me, the most vivid picture comes from a coffee percolator. The water goes up a small tube and drains down through the coffee grounds. After enough cycles, the flavor of the coffee beans has been transferred to the water which we then call coffee. So it is that we need to cycle our thoughts through the "grounds" of God's Word until we start to think like God and then act godly or godlike.

Scripture commands that we meditate in three areas:

1. *God* ....Psalm 27:4; 63:3
2. *God's Word* ....Joshua 1:8; Psalm 1:2
3. *God's works* ....Psalm 143:5, 145:5

The greatest portion of Scripture that talks about Scripture is Psalm 119. All 176 verses extol the virtue of knowing and living out the mind of God. Meditation is mentioned at least seven times as the habit of one who loves God and desires a closer intimacy with Him: "O how I love Thy law! It is my meditation all the day.... My eyes anticipate the night watches, that I may meditate on Thy word" (Ps. 119:97, 148; see also vv. 15, 23, 48, 78, 99).

You can "chew" on God's Word as you read it daily and you also can think about it during other times when your mind is free. That requires that you internalize the Word or be able to recall what you have read.

However you do it, meditating on God's Word will cleanse away the old thoughts that are not of God. Meditation places and reinforces new thoughts from Scripture. Also, it puts a protective shield around your mind to reject incoming thoughts that contradict God. That's the scriptural process of renewing your mind.

Turning On the Light

Scripture tells us that we need God's help to understand God's Word.

Now we have received, not the spirit of the world, but the Spirit who is from God, that we might know the things freely given to us by God, which things we also speak, not in words taught by human wisdom, but in those taught by

*the Spirit, combining spiritual thoughts with spiritual
words (1 Cor. 2:12-13).*

Theologians call this "illumination." We use the expres-
sions, "It just dawned on me" or "The light just came on" to
describe darkened thoughts which later take on new understanding. God's Spirit does that for us with Scripture.

One of my favorite and most often uttered prayers as I
study Scripture is, "Open my eyes, that I may behold wonderful things from Thy law" (Ps. 119:18). It acknowledges
that I need God's light in Scripture. So do verses like, "Teach
me, O Lord, the way of Thy statutes, and I shall observe it to
the end. Give me understanding, that I may observe Thy law,
and keep it with all my heart" (vv. 33-34; see also v. 102).

God wants us to know and understand and obey. So He
gives us all the help we need through His Holy Spirit. We,
like the men to whom Jesus spoke on the road to Emmaus,
need God's help: "Then He opened their minds to understand the Scriptures" (Luke 24:45).

Christ's Mind

Ultimately and immediately, we must think like Christ. According to Paul, God gave us a good start: "For who has
known the mind of the Lord, that he should instruct Him?
But we have the mind of Christ" (1 Cor. 2:16).

Possessing Christ's mind obligates us to use Christ's mind.
So Paul writes to the Philippians, "Have this attitude [mind]
in yourselves which was also in Christ Jesus" (Phil. 2:5).
What does that involve? Christ's mind led Him to:

1. Sacrifice (Phil. 2:7).
2. Submit (Phil. 2:8).

So we, like Christ, need to think in terms of what we can
give, not what we can receive; of how we can obey, not how
we can rebel. One who gives and obeys will be a servant, just
like Christ. Such is the lifestyle of the person who thinks
"sacrifice" and "submission."

Satan's Attack

To be forewarned is to be forearmed. While a commitment to think Christianly sounds great, it is not without opposition. For Satan would have you think contrary to God's Word and then act disobediently to God's will.[3]

Understand first that before you became a Christian your mind was blinded by the devil: "The god of this world has blinded the minds of the unbelieving, that they might not see the light of the gospel of the glory of Christ, who is the image of God" (2 Cor. 4:4).

Even after salvation, Satan continues his intellectual rampage. Paul had a great concern for the Corinthian church, for he writes, "But I am afraid, lest as the serpent deceived Eve by his craftiness, your minds should be led astray from the simplicity and purity of devotion to Christ" (11:3).

Eve had allowed Satan to do some thinking for her. Then she did some of her own thinking independent of God. When her conclusions differed from God's, she chose to act on hers not God's, which is sin (Gen. 3:1-7).

In warning believers about the battle with Satan, Paul on two occasions tells about the schemes or wiles of the devil. Two different Greek words are used, but they both refer to the mind:

Put on the full armor of God, that you may be able to stand firm against the schemes of the devil (Eph. 6:11).

In order that no advantage be taken of us by Satan, for we are not ignorant of his schemes (2 Cor. 2:11).

No one is immune from this kind of attack. Even the Apostle Peter succumbed. Remember the Lord's words of rebuke: "Get behind Me, Satan! You are a stumbling block to Me; for you are not setting your mind on God's interests, but man's" (Matt. 16:23).

So you really do need to heed Peter's strong encouragement to "gird your mind for action, keep sober in Spirit, fix your hope completely on the grace to be brought to you at the revelation of Jesus Christ" (1 Peter 1:13). You'll do that by thinking like God.

Think on These Things

Someone has said that the mind is the taproot of the soul. That being so, we need to carefully and nutritiously feed our soul by sinking our taproot deep into God's mind in Scripture. So we ask, "What's the recommended soul food?"

Paul's gourmet menu for the mind includes those things which are:
1. True
2. Honorable
3. Right
4. Pure
5. Lovely
6. Of good repute
7. Excellent
8. Praiseworthy

We must dwell on these sorts of things with our minds (Phil. 4:8). Where do we find these kinds of thoughts? In the Bible! A book of God's word, containing God's will for God's people.

All Scripture is inspired by God and profitable for teaching, for reproof, for correction, for training in righteousness; that the man of God may be adequately equipped for every good work (2 Tim. 3:16-17).

The Bottom Line

You might be asking, "What will I gain?" God anticipated your question. Carefully consider His answer.

This book of the law shall not depart from your mouth, but you shall meditate on it day and night, so that you may be careful to do according to all that is written in it; for then you will make your way prosperous, and then you will have success (Josh. 1:8).

How blessed is the man who does not walk in the counsel of the wicked, nor stand in the path of sinners, nor sit in the seat of scoffers! But his delight is in the law of the Lord, and in His law he meditates day and night. And he will be like a tree firmly planted by streams of water, which yields its fruit in its season, and its leaf does not wither; and in whatever he does, he prospers (Ps. 1:1-3).

When you think like God wants you to think and act like God wants you to act, then you will receive God's blessing for obedience. Spiritually, you will be that obedient child, that pure bride, that healthy sheep in Christ's flock who experiences the greatest intimacy with God.

It's amazing how scholars and philosophers over the centuries have recognized the importance of the mind but have rejected the Creator of the mind and the Saviour of the soul. Charles Colson lets us look in on one such classic case:

It was cold and raw that day in 1610 when a French mathematician named Rene Descartes pulled his cloak around him and climbed into the side compartment of a large stove. Descartes had been wrestling for weeks with questions of doubt and reason in his search for some certainty of a philosophical system. As he warmed himself in his stove, his imagination began glowing with the light of reason, and he resolved to doubt everything that could possibly be doubted.

Hours later Descartes emerged, having determined that there was only one thing he could not doubt, and that was the fact that he doubted. A good day's work. Descartes drew the conclusion, Cogito, ergo sum: *"I think, therefore I am." Then he went out for a cognac.*

Descartes' now-famous postulate led to a whole new

promise for philosophic thought: man, rather than God, became the fixed point around which everything else revolved; human reason became the foundation upon which a structure of knowledge could be built; and doubt became the highest intellectual value.[4]

The ultimate form of idolatry would be, like Descartes, to reject the mind of God and worship at the altar of our own independent thinking. Our greatest intimacy with the Lord will be those times when His thoughts supersede ours and our behavior then models the behavior of Christ.

We are what we think. That exact idea came from the proverbist's pen close to 3,000 years ago (Prov. 23:7). This truth can be lived out for good or for evil. If we choose to think like God, then we will act like Him. I commend this mental and spiritual route to you with the same enthusiasm as the psalmist:

O how I love Thy law!
It is my meditation all the day.
Thy commandments make me wiser than my enemies,
For they are ever mine.
I have more insight than all my teachers,
For Thy testimonies are my meditation.
I understand more than the aged,
Because I have observed Thy precepts.
I have restrained my feet from every evil way,
That I may keep Thy word.
I have not turned aside from Thine ordinances,
For Thou Thyself hast taught me.
How sweet are Thy words to my taste!
Yes, sweeter than honey to my mouth!
From Thy precepts I get understanding;
Therefore I hate every false way.

Psalm 119:97-104

I said to the Lord, "Thou art my God;
Give ear, O Lord,
to the voice of my supplications."
Psalm 140:6

4
TALKING TO GOD

An executive received notification that he would be transferred to another part of the country. His young daughter, having lived her entire life where they were, became unhappy over the pending move.

The night before the moving van arrived she said her evening prayers. She went through the usual "God bless Mommy and Daddy," then added, "I guess I'd better tell You too, God, that this is good-bye. I won't be able to pray to You anymore—we're moving to New York."

For many the mere mention of prayer produces thoughts of awkwardness, inadequacy, or embarrassment. At times, we feel as infantlike in prayer as the young girl who didn't want to move.

Or perhaps we're like the two middle-aged men who had been neighbors as farm boys and met one day on a city street. They reminisced for a few minutes, then agreed to meet again and visit their boyhood homes. The time came and they began to stroll through the fields, eventually coming to a pasture where a herd of cattle was grazing. They passed through a barbed-wire fence into the field, unafraid of the cattle.

As they walked further, a bull suddenly appeared, snorting and pawing. The men started running back toward the fence and the bull gave chase. When they realized they were not going to reach the fence in time, one man said, "We'd better start praying," and then, since both were unaccustomed to praying, he added, "You had a father that prayed, or that at least said table grace, so you know more about praying than I do." So quickly the other man said the only prayer he could remember: "O Lord, let us be thankful for that which we are about to receive!"

We're all at times guilty of praying only in emergencies, of turning to God only when the heat is on.

But what is the true essence of prayer? Ray Stedman explains prayer as an awareness of our helpless need and an acknowledgment of divine adequacy![1] Put more simply, prayer is the conversation between a spiritual child with his or her Heavenly Father.

It can be praise and thanksgiving, praying for someone (intercession) or praying for yourself (supplication), a confession of sin or a request for a specific need (petition). Whatever our prayer, we come to God as helpless paupers seeking His divine resources for our lives.

Biblical Keys

From the first to the last, biblical prayer marks the connecting link from man to God. Joshua prayed and the sun stood still (Josh. 10:12-13). Nehemiah prayed that the king would grant his request (Neh. 2:4). And Daniel prayed for God's deliverance of Israel (Dan. 9:4-19).

Jesus prayed constantly (Luke 3:21; 5:16; 6:12; 9:18, 28; 11:1; 22:32, 41). He never taught His disciples how to preach but He did instruct them how to pray (11:1-4). Paul constantly prayed for those whom he loved (1 Thes. 1:2-3). Prayer, perhaps more than any other activity, measures the level of intimacy we have with the Lord.

Charles Spurgeon suggested that prayer is the slender nerve that moves the muscle of God's omnipotence. We need to know how that works; how we can pray in such a way that God hears and answers.

Some have believed it is the special words or phrases we use. Others believe it is the closing of eyes or the folding of hands or kneeling on knees. The place of prayer has been suggested as the key to success. But that's not what the Bible teaches.

Prayer rises above the externals. It is based on what is inside of us, not mere words or ways. There are five biblical keys to fruitful prayer revealed in Scripture. They are:

1. Our willingness to give (James 4:1-3).
2. Our willingness to believe (James 1:5-8).
3. Our willingness to yield (1 John 5:14-15).
4. Our willingness to obey (1 John 3:22).
5. Our willingness to wait (Luke 18:1-8).

Right Reasons

Selfish prayer does not commend itself to God. Note these words in James' epistle:

> *What is the source of quarrels and conflicts among you? Is not the source your pleasures that wage war in your members? You lust and do not have; so you commit murder. And you are envious and cannot obtain; so you fight and quarrel. You do not have because you do not ask. You ask and do not receive, because you ask with wrong motives, so that you may spend it on your pleasures (James 4:1-3).*

That early church dealt with internal strife every step of the way (4:1). Jesus taught unity; they experienced division. Why? Selfishness. These Christians lived a self-centered existence rather than focusing chiefly on God and others.

They grabbed for what they wanted and usually came up empty-handed. To their plight James responds, "You do not have because you do not ask" (4:2). They had long ago left God out of the process.

But some did pray. However, they prayed with the same failure to receive. These asked or prayed for wrong reasons. Self-gratification and self-satisfaction drove their prayers. They possessed little concern for the kingdom of God or the household of their Heavenly Father.

If you are a parent, you can understand this better than most. If your children come with various requests, which one will you be more likely to honor? The kid who is always concerned with himself or the child who has your best interest and those of other family members in mind?

Does that mean it's wrong to pray for yourself? No! It does mean, however, that you need to ask *why* you are making a certain request of God. Here is a quick test:

1. Is this request reflecting that I am first and foremost in my life seeking God's kingdom and His righteousness? (Matt. 6:33)

2. Am I considering other people to be more important than me? (Phil. 2:3)

Take a moment to recall Jesus' account of the Pharisee and the tax collector as they prayed (Luke 18:9-14). The first prayed to justify himself; the second, to be justified by God. This most vividly illustrates the importance of praying with right motives.

Your attitude proves far more important than your ability to articulate a masterful prayer. Perhaps the simplicity of this child would be best. Her grandfather overheard her repeating the alphabet in reverent, hushed tones. "What are you doing?" he inquired. "I'm praying, Grandpa," she replied. "I can't think of the right words, so I just say all the letters. God will put them together for me because He knows what I'm thinking."

Right Rest

A prayer without faith resembles a car without an engine—
they both go nowhere. Without faith it is impossible to please
God (Heb. 11:6). Also, without faith it is impossible to reach
God in prayer.

> *But if any of you lacks wisdom, let him ask of God, who
> gives to all men generously and without reproach, and it
> will be given to him. But let him ask in faith without any
> doubting, for the one who doubts is like the surf of the sea
> driven and tossed by the wind (James 1:5-7).*

To pray without faith is to question either God's existence,
His ability, or His willingness. When we pray, it must be with
the confidence that God is, that He is able, and that He does
all things perfectly.

Faith willingly accepts God's denial of a request and be-
lieves that God has a better idea. The early church accepted
James' death although they most certainly had prayed for his
release as they later prayed for Peter's (Acts 12:1-2, 12). Paul
accepted his thorn in the flesh in spite of praying for its
removal (2 Cor. 12:7-10).

Faith can then embrace God's delivery of answered prayer.
Those who had prayed so faithfully for James surely were
disappointed. But think of the delight when Peter, for whom
they had also prayed in exactly the same circumstances,
showed up as living proof that God intervened (Acts 12:5, 16-
17).

Warren Wiersbe relates four levels of prayer. In a sense,
they each reflect a growing maturity of faith.

1. Grade school level—praying.
2. High school level—praying for God's will.
3. College level—praying as children to their Heavenly
   Father.
4. Post-graduate level—praying for spiritual maturity.

Which level best describes your prayer life?

Right Realm

Over a century ago Richard Chenevix Trench crisply wrote, "Prayer is not overcoming God's reluctance; it is laying hold of His willingness." Almost 2,000 years ago John recorded these words:

> And this is the confidence which we have before Him, that, if we ask anything according to His will, He hears us. And if we know that He hears us in whatever we ask, we know that we have the requests which we have asked from Him (1 John 5:14-15).

God's will frames effective prayer. Central to Christ's teaching of prayer came this principle:

> Thy Kingdom come. Thy will be done, on earth as it is in heaven (Matt. 6:10).

Central to Christ's praying came this practice:

> And He went a little beyond them, and fell on His face and prayed, saying, "My Father, if it is possible, let this cup pass from Me; yet not as I will, but as Thou wilt" (Matt. 26:39).

The essence of prayer does not involve satisfying our personal wishes, but rather being so changed by our communion with God that we come to wholeheartedly crave His will for us. The psalmist put it this way, "Delight yourself in the Lord; and He will give you the desires of your heart" (Ps. 37:4).

Right Response

As a parent, will you be more inclined to respond to the obedient or disobedient child? Ponder God's response to His spiritual children:

*If I regard wickedness in my heart, the Lord will not hear
(Ps. 66:18).*

*And whatever we ask we receive from Him, because we
keep His commandments and do the things that are pleasing in His sight (1 John 3:22).*

Let me illustrate from Scripture. Daniel proved to be the
epitome of obedience. Even though he had not yet passed out
of adolescence—and despite the fact that he had been violent-
ly separated from his parents and forced to live in a pagan
culture—he still clung to an uncompromising allegiance to
God (Dan. 1:8-9). It's no wonder that when Daniel stood on
the brink of death and prayed, God delivered him (2:18-23).
This sort of experience marked the remainder of Daniel's life.
He prayed for release from the lions' den and God delivered
(6:10, 22-23). He also prayed for the release of Israel from
foreign domination and God answered (9:3-19).

Israel, on the other hand, often proved that God meant
business when He said He would not honor disobedience.

*Behold, the Lord's hand is not so short that it cannot save;
neither is His ear so dull that it cannot hear. But your
iniquities have made a separation between you and your
God, and your sins have hidden His face from you, so that
He does not hear. For your hands are defiled with blood,
and your fingers with iniquity; your lips have spoken false-
hood, your tongue mutters wickedness (Isa. 59:1-3).*

The more time you spend listening to God in His Word,
the more likely you will talk to God in prayer. With growing
intimacy comes increased obedience.

A.T. Pierson paints this vivid picture of intimacy:

He who would keep up intimate converse with the Lord

*must habitually find in the Scriptures the highway of such
companionship. God's aristocracy, His nobility, the princes
of His realm are not the wise, mighty, and highborn of
earth, but often the poor, weak, despised of men, who abide
in His presence, and devoutly commune with Him through
His inspired Word. Blessed are they who have thus learned
to use the key which gives free access, not only to the King's
treasures, but to the King Himself.*[2]

Right Restraint

Impatience mocks God, who always sets the absolute, precise
standard of time. The psalmist struggled with waiting (Ps.
13:1-2). Saul's unwillingness to wait led to his fall from Israel's throne (1 Sam. 13:1-14). The disciples were always in a
hurry (Acts 1:6).

That tendency must be the reason behind our Lord's parable of the nasty judge and needy widow (Luke 18:1-8). It
begins: "Now He was telling them a parable to show that at
all times they ought to pray and not to lose heart" (v. 1).

Delay does not mean denial. God just has a better timeta-
ble. Pray until God shows you that you are to stop.

No better example of this could be found than in the prayer
life of Zacharias and Elizabeth. One day in the twilight moments of his priestly career, Zacharias ministered in the temple and heard an angel say, "Do not be afraid, Zacharias, for
your petition has been heard" (Luke 1:13). What petition?
Obviously the prayer for a child (vv. 13-14).

This great news shocked Zacharias, who asked, "How shall
I know of this for certain? For I am an old man, and my wife
is advanced in years" (v. 18).

Imagine praying for years that God would bless your marital union with a child, knowing that society would conclude
barrenness meant God's displeasure. Then, when you and
your spouse were past child-bearing years, you accepted
God's will of no child. So you planned to finish out your
career and retire. Now in the waning days of your service,

you discover the baby is on the way. That describes Zacharias' experience perfectly.

In your prayer, be persistent and be patient. But above all, be prepared!

Plan of Attack

Here are some simple steps to take as you launch out on a lifetime journey of prayer:

Admission—*Lord, I am unable!*
Submission—*Lord, You know best!*
Transmission—*Lord, please intervene!*
Intermission—*Lord, I will wait for You!*
Permission—*Lord, thank You for Your answer!*

The psalmists prayed at least twenty times, "Lord, be gracious/merciful to me/us." That's a great place to start and to end in your prayer life.

Parting Thoughts

Ultimately, the greatest blessing of prayer is not in receiving the answer, but rather in becoming the kind of intimate friend whom God can trust with the answer. Listen to the psalmist's words: "But certainly God has heard; He has given heed to the voice of my prayer. Blessed be God, who has not turned away my prayer, nor His lovingkindness from me" (Ps. 66:19-20).

Prayer undoubtedly proves to be the greatest opportunity a believer can enter into. Note these two New Testament promises:

Let us therefore draw near with confidence to the throne of grace, that we may receive mercy and may find grace to help in time of need (Heb. 4:16).

Now to Him who is able to do exceeding abundantly beyond

all that we ask or think, according to the power that works within us (Eph. 3:20).

One night a British soldier was caught creeping back into his quarters from the nearby woods. He was taken before his commanding officer and charged with holding communications with the enemy. The man pleaded that he had gone into the woods to be alone to pray. That was his only defense.

"Have you been in the habit of spending hours in private prayer?" the officer growled.

"Yes, sir!"

"Then down on your knees and pray now! You never needed it so much!"

Expecting immediate death, the soldier knelt down and poured out his soul in prayer that could only be inspired by the power of the Holy Spirit.

"You may go," said the officer simply, when the soldier had finished. "I believe your story. If you hadn't drilled often, you could not do so well at review."

How well would you have done?

STEP TWO

"GROWING TOGETHER"

*But speaking the truth in love,
we are to grow up in all aspects into Him,
who is the head, even Christ.*
Ephesians 4:15

*But grow in the grace and knowledge
of our Lord and Saviour Jesus Christ.
To Him be the glory, both now
and to the day of eternity. Amen.*
2 Peter 3:18

*I feel like a man who has no money in his pocket
but is allowed to draw for all he wants upon
one infinitely rich; I am, therefore, at once
both a beggar and a rich man.*[1]
John Newton

I was glad when they said to me,
"Let us go to the house of the Lord."
Psalm 122:1

5
WORSHIPING GOD

A well-known worship leader, commenting on contemporary worship in America, said in my presence recently, "People play at their worship, worship their work, and work at their play." How tragic—how true!

If any one of these major life activities—worship, work, or play—falls prey to error, then the other two will likely be affected also. So it's imperative that we understand God's desire for our spiritual activities, sustaining energies, and social outlets.

Obviously, worship becomes the place to begin since God is our highest priority. Our word *worship* originated with the Anglo-Saxon *weoscrip,* meaning "that to which we ascribe worth or value." In a religious sense, it can be directed to an unlimited number of created objects or persons. However, in a biblical context, worship ascribes ultimate eternal worth to God alone; and that is why God jealously demands to be the exclusive object of worship.

You shall not make for yourself an idol, or any likeness of what is in heaven above or on the earth beneath or in the water under the earth. You shall not worship them or serve them; for I, the Lord your God, am a jealous God, visiting the iniquity of the fathers on the children, on the third and fourth generations of those who hate Me, but showing loving-kindness to thousands, to those who love Me and keep My commandments (Ex. 20:4-6).

Scripturally, the prominent Hebrew and Greek terms translated "worship" derive from the ancient practice of bowing oneself to the ground as an outward sign of reverence. In a broad sense, then, worship expresses the recognition and celebration that God is the one, true, eternal Sovereign upon whom we are totally dependent and to whom we ascribe absolute spiritual allegiance.

True worship can be personal and corporate, but true corporate worship will always be preceded by the personal side. Worship can be either outward or inward; authentic outward expression will always be validated by a true inward attitude.

For our immediate purpose, let me broadly define worship as living in the presence of God according to His will for His pleasure and glory. Put another way, it is having spiritual fellowship with God (1 John 1:3).

God's Plan
One of the common threads running from Genesis to Revelation is God's desire to "tabernacle" among His people and to be their God. The fellowship between God and man began in the Garden of Eden, but quickly disintegrated because Adam's sin erected a barrier between God and the human race. Both Adam and Eve were evicted from Eden where they previously had walked and talked with God.

The Lord reaffirmed His desire to fellowship with man by initiating a relationship with Israel. He visibly demonstrated this relationship by displaying His Shekinah presence in Moses' tabernacle and Solomon's temple.

> *Moreover, I will make My dwelling among you, and My soul will not reject you. I will also walk among you and be your God, and you shall be My people (Lev. 26:11-12).*

But God's dwelling among Israel, similar to Eden, ended due to sin on the part of Israel (Ezek. 10–11).

This tabernacling of God now takes place individually as He dwells within those who are His in Christ: "Do you not know that you are a temple of God, and that the Spirit of God dwells in you?" (1 Cor. 3:16)

For Christians who die, the tabernacle experience continues in heaven where Christ now sits at God the Father's right hand.

> *Now the main point in what has been said is this: we have such a high priest, who has taken His seat at the right hand of the throne of the Majesty in the heavens, a minister in the sanctuary, and in the true tabernacle, which the Lord pitched, not man (Heb. 8:1-2; see also 9:23-24).*

The Tribulation martyrs likewise may look forward to a heavenly tabernacle.

> *For this reason, they are before the throne of God; and they serve Him day and night in His temple; and He who sits on the throne shall spread His tabernacle over them (Rev. 7:15).*

The inhabitants of the earth during the Millennium will take up where Israel left off.

> *And I will make a covenant of peace with them; it will be an everlasting covenant with them. And I will place them and multiply them, and will set My sanctuary in their*

midst forever. My dwelling place also will be with them; and I will be their God, and they will be My people. And the nations will know that I am the Lord who sanctifies Israel, when My sanctuary is in their midst forever (Ezek. 37:26-28).

Finally, eternity future involves the perfect expression and experience of God fulfilling His forever purpose of ruling over and dwelling among His people.

And I heard a loud voice from the throne, saying, "Behold, the tabernacle of God is among men, and He shall dwell among them, and they shall be His people, and God Himself shall be among them" (Rev. 21:3).

Man's Past

As with Adam and Eve in Eden and Israel at the Shekinah's departure, sin disrupts the worship communion between human beings and God. Yet man persistently tries to restore the broken relationship according to his own wisdom. Three forms of bankrupt worship emerge from worship as defined by man.

1. Idolatrous worship involving wrong gods with a wrong heart.

And he did away with idolatrous priests whom the kings of Judah had appointed to burn incense in the high places in the cities of Judah and in the surrounding area of Jerusalem, also those who burned incense to Baal, to the sun and to the moon and to the constellations and to all the host of heaven (2 Kings 23:5).

2. Ignorant worship involving wrong gods with a sincere heart.

For while I was passing through and examining the objects

of your worship, I also found an altar with this inscription, "TO THE UNKNOWN GOD." What therefore you worship in ignorance, this I proclaim to you (Acts 17:23).

3. Vain worship involving the true God but with a wrong heart attitude.

This people honors Me with their lips, but their heart is far away from Me. But in vain do they worship Me, teaching as doctrines the precepts of man (Matt. 15:8-9).

Satan craves to be worshiped, but should always be denied (Isa. 14:13-14; Matt. 4:8-10). Man inclines to worship angels, but they always reject it (Rev. 19:10; 22:8-9). Humans try to worship other human beings (Acts 10:25; 14:11-15). Paul summarizes the human race's sinful inclination to render worship to someone other than God: "For they exchanged the truth of God for a lie, and worshiped and served the creature rather than the Creator, who is blessed forever. Amen" (Rom. 1:25).

Only one kind of right worship ever existed—worship in spirit and in truth. "God is spirit, and those who worship Him must worship in spirit and truth" (John 4:24).

True worship involves the spiritual realm and is always in accord with God's truth concerning both the object and means of worship.

The Bible records many true worship experiences such as:

Abraham and Isaac	Gen. 22:5ff
Eliezer	Gen. 24:26
Israel in Egypt	Ex. 4:31
Joshua	Josh. 5:14-15
Gideon	Jud. 7:15
David	2 Sam. 12:20
Ezra	Neh. 8:6; 9:3
Job	Job 1:20
Wise men	Matt. 2:11

Blind man . . . . .John 9:38
Angels . . . . .Heb. 1:6

But the most personal and detailed is the experience of Isaiah.

Personal Worship

Prophets normally preach. In one instance, however, Isaiah found himself in the pew, not the pulpit. From his memorable experience, he teaches us about the key elements in the dynamics of true worship.

Whether by personal choice or God's sovereign will, Isaiah found himself gazing on God's uncluttered glory.

In the year of King Uzziah's death, I saw the Lord sitting on a throne, lofty and exalted, with the train of His robe filling the temple. Seraphim stood above Him, each having six wings; with two he covered his face, and with two he covered his feet, and with two he flew. And one called out to another and said, "Holy, Holy, Holy, is the Lord of hosts, the whole earth is full of His glory." And the foundations of the thresholds trembled at the voice of him who called out, while the temple was filling with smoke (Isa. 6:1-4).

The significance of this beginning step of worship can be best understood in the historical context of the times.

1. King Uzziah had acted corruptly with regard to temple worship and God had struck him down with leprosy (2 Chron. 26:19-20).
2. Despite this judgment, the people continued to act corruptly (2 Chron. 27:2).

Although Jotham ruled well for sixteen years following his father Uzziah's death, God knew that Israel's prophet needed a fresh glimpse of God's glory and holiness to sustain him in spiritually turbulent times. The same is true for us.

In the midst of God's perfect presence, Isaiah remembered how unholy he was by contrast. He confessed his own sinfulness and Israel's, crying out for God's mercy with a deep sense of need for spiritual cleansing: "Woe is me, for I am ruined! Because I am a man of unclean lips, and I live among a people of unclean lips; for my eyes have seen the King, the Lord of hosts" (Isa. 6:5).

Isaiah 6:6-7 portrays God's cleansing and forgiveness which the prophet sought. The worship experience — standing in God's presence — brought Isaiah once more to the realization that the Lord reigns supreme in heaven and on earth. Apparently Isaiah had become too bogged down in earthly circumstances (the king's death) and not attentive enough to God's promises and presence. For Isaiah that was sin.

With a freshness of soul and a renewed sense of God's magnificence, Isaiah responded to God's call for service with a new burst of energy.

Then I heard the voice of the Lord, saying, "Whom shall I send, and who will go for us?" Then I said, "Here am I. Send me!" (Isa. 6:8)

Four elements stand out in Isaiah's worship experience which should be applicable for us on a daily basis.
1. Seeing God's holiness and glory through Scripture.
2. Sensing the need to be clean and holy for unhindered fellowship with God.
3. Seizing God's promise for forgiveness.
4. Serving God with obedience.

Corporate Worship
Since eternity will be spent worshiping God, we should be practicing now for the future. What will worship in heaven be like?

Revelation 4–5 paints the most vivid and active picture of heavenly worship in Scripture. What we perceive in heaven should be at the heart of our practice on earth. Six observations prove especially important to shape our worship.

Observation 1—Worship is the exclusive activity. The scenes in both Revelation 4 and 5 conclude with a summary statement about worship:

The twenty-four elders will fall down before Him who sits on the throne, and will worship Him who lives forever and ever, and will cast their crowns before the throne (4:10).

And the four living creatures kept saying, "Amen." And the elders fell down and worshiped (5:14).

Observation 2—God is the exclusive focus of worship. The Father (4:2, 9-11), the Son (5:5-6), and the Holy Spirit (4:5; 5:6) all feature prominently in the scene. The object and attention of worship is not the congregation, the pastor, the musician, or peripheral features. Worship that is centered anywhere and upon anyone other than God alone is not true worship.

Observation 3—Praise for God laces the worship of heaven. On at least five occasions the participants burst forth with adoration—4:8; 4:9-11; 5:9-10; 5:12; and 5:13.

Observation 4—Truth about God provides the context of worship. Not sermonettes that entertain, not platitudes that produce goosebumps, but reality about God that changes lives marks heavenly worship.

The character of God (4:8), the creation (4:11), God's sovereignty (4:11), salvation (5:9, 12), and the kingdom (5:10) comprise the truth touched upon. This feature expresses itself as preaching in our earthly worship.

Observation 5—All of God's living entourage united in worship. The four living creatures (4:6-8; 5:8; 5:14), the multitude of angels (5:11), and redeemed humanity represented by the twenty-four elders (4:4; 5:8; 5:14) all joined in corporate worship of God.

Observation 6—The essence of heavenly worship provides the model for earthly worship.

Thy kingdom come, Thy will be done, on earth as it is in heaven (Matt. 6:10).

Corporate worship will flesh out differently in separate congregations and on different occasions. But these six elements should always be the framework of true corporate worship.

One final thought. No greater experience of worship comes than at times of baptism, which celebrates new life and salvation (Matt. 28:19) and the reproduction of the Upper Room experience, which celebrates Christ's death and its results (John 13:17). These always prove to be blessed times of family worship in the local church.

Contemporary Practice

Personal worship is always appropriate; but what about corporate worship? When should the church gather?

The early church placed special prominence upon the first day of the week for worship (Acts 20:7; 1 Cor. 16:2; Rev. 1:10) because that was the day of Christ's resurrection. Here are some additional reasons for Sunday to be a day of corporate worship. In our culture:

1. It provides the only opportunity during the week for the entire flock to hear the heart, mind, and voice of the Senior Shepherd.
2. It's the only opportunity during the week for God's flock to join their hearts together in unified worship.
3. It's the only time during the week that the flock can blend their voices in one praise together to God.
4. It's the only time during the week to join hands in giving sacrificially to the Lord.
5. It's the only opportunity during the week in which the congregation (both young and old) can have a common shared experience.
6. It's the only time during the week in which the large body can be in a position to encourage and stimulate one

another to love and good deeds in accord with Hebrews 10:24-25.

As believers come together to worship, two factors intersect: first, the dynamics of the individual person who prepares and anticipates worship; second, the joining together of likeminded worshipers. Let's focus for a moment on preparation and anticipation.

Externals alone have very little to do with true worship. Only a heart and mind totally devoted to Almighty God can go beyond the "letter of worship" and fully enter into the authentic "spirit of worship" that God's holiness demands.

A renewed sense of worship begins each Lord's Day as believers gather to celebrate the greatness of God and the wonderful hope of eternal life in Jesus Christ. This time should set a true worshiper's focus on the glory of God and help to maintain this heavenly perspective throughout the week.

In order to most highly honor God and to prepare yourself for exalting worship, carefully consider the following questions. Every time you prepare to worship, work through them to make sure that you are fully ready to commune with our great God. You might want to tuck these thoughts away in the front of your Bible for easy reference.

1. Am I coming before God to worship Him with a sincere heart? (Heb. 10:22)
2. Am I focusing my full attention on the Lord alone? (Ex. 20:4-6)
3. Am I coming to worship as a true child of the Heavenly Father, knowing that my sins are cleansed through personal faith in the Lord Jesus Christ? (Rom. 10:9-13)
4. Am I coming with a firm grip on the confession of our hope in Jesus Christ? (Heb. 4:14-16)
5. Am I fixing my sight on the Lord of glory in His Word so that my hungering desire is to draw near to Him? (Heb. 7:25; James 4:8)

6. Am I coming with the full assurance that faith provides a sufficient entrance into God's presence—before His throne of grace? (Heb. 11:6)

7. Am I coming to God with the knowledge that the only reason which allows for the privilege of worship is what Christ did for me at Calvary? (Matt. 27:51; 1 Tim. 2:5)

8. Am I coming in purity—cleansed from the daily sin in my life? (1 John 1:9)

9. Am I coming to render honor, glory, praise, and thanksgiving to God rather than to receive anything for myself? (1 Cor. 10:31)

10. Am I praying that, having entered into the presence of God through worship, He will break me, mold me, and make me a pure vessel, useful for the Master's service? (2 Tim. 2:21)

A Testimony

Worship involves the highest privilege and the most exalted of experiences. It is at the apex of Christian living. Worship fuels intimacy with God and heightens our commitment to God's kingdom purpose.

Worship wears appropriately well in all seasons of life—whether one experiences catastrophe like Job (Job 1:13-22) or celebration like Hezekiah (2 Chron. 29:1-30).

One of the psalmists leaves us this legacy expressing his sublime delight over the prospect of worship.

How lovely are Thy dwelling places, O Lord of hosts!
My soul longed and even yearned for the courts of the Lord;
my heart and my flesh sing for joy to the living God.
The bird also has found a house, and the swallow a nest
for herself, where she may lay her young, even Thine altars,
O Lord of hosts, my King and my God.
How blessed are those who dwell in Thy house!
They are ever praising Thee (Ps. 84:1-4).

I will bless the Lord at all times;
His praise shall continually be in my mouth.
Psalm 34:1

6
PRAISING GOD

I vividly remember the dramatic impact this letter had on me when I first read it. My praise life has never been the same.

I spent one and a half years on a kidney machine before getting a transplant. At first I did a lot of complaining, like everyone else. Then one day I stopped all the complaining when I read the account of the Crucifixion.

In the kidney center they helped me get out of my coat; with Jesus they stripped off His robe. When entering the kidney center, the nurses would always speak a kind word to me. But Jesus heard, "Crucify Him."

Sometimes on the machine I would develop a headache. They would give me something for it and bring me an ice pack for comfort. Jesus got a crown of thorns. Sometimes I would get thirsty and they would bring me juice and ice water. But Jesus got vinegar and gall. I laid on a comfortable bed for four or five hours, but Jesus hung on a cross.

*I hardly felt the needle they put in my arm, but He had
nails painfully driven through His hands and feet. My
blood was cleansed and recirculated, but His ran out on
the ground.*

*Jesus had turned my days of complaining into days of
praising. A careful look into the events that took place that
day on Calvary should stop all our complaining. If only we
would look in that direction.*[1]

He Alone Is Worthy

The '70s and '80s brought a revolution in worship music.
Choruses popped up everywhere, abounding with Scripture
and focusing on God. Praise music arrived with the simplicity
of an "Alleluia" and the grandeur of "My Tribute" or "Majesty." Both the music and the lyrics seemed to catapult Christians closer to God's presence.

Every major change finds its critics and praise music
proved no exception. Much criticism came unwarranted, but
some was deserved and profitable, in hopes that the spiritual
blessings that praise music restored to the Christian community would not be spoiled by its excesses.

Often the "spiritual high" received from the music over-
shadowed its purpose. People at times praised "praise" rather than God. The phrase "Praise the Lord" grew so common
that it became an unthinking response rather than true worship. God must remain the purpose and object of all our
praise or it will possess no spiritual value.

But praise music did not originate with our generation.
Let's turn to Scripture's praise music. It's mainly found in the
Psalms. Recently, with the marvel of computers, I looked at
the over 260 Scripture references to praise at one sitting.
One of my overwhelming impressions from that study was
that God is *the* object of praise. Almost always praise divided
itself among the name of God, the Word of God, the character
of God, and the works of God. This then should be our praise
pattern—always God-focused.

God's name. Here's just a sample: "Let them praise Thy great and awesome name; holy is He" (Ps. 99:3); "Let them praise the name of the Lord, for His name alone is exalted" (148:13; see also 7:17; 9:2; 69:30; 145:2).

We can praise Him as Elohim, the sovereignly supreme God, or with the name Jehovah (LORD); the eternal God. We can praise His power and strength by calling Him El-Shaddai or God Almighty (Gen. 17:1-2). One of the more popular praise songs has been "He Is Lord" or Adonai, which exalts God as Master over all.

In the Old Testament, the name Jehovah has several variations, all of which prove praiseworthy.[2]

- *Jehovah-jireh: provider (Gen. 22:14)*
- *Jehovah-rophe: healer (Ex. 15:26)*
- *Jehovah-nissi: banner (Ex. 17:15)*
- *Jehovah-shalom: peace (Jud. 6:24)*
- *Jehovah-tsidkenu: righteousness (Jer. 23:6)*
- *Jehovah-rohi: shepherd (Ps. 23:1)*
- *Jehovah-shammah: presence (Ezek. 48:35)*
- *Jehovah-m'kaddesh: sanctifier (Lev. 20:8)*

God's Word. The Lord's "love letter" to His people is something that should always elicit our praise. The psalmist certainly thought so.

In God, whose word I praise, in God I have put my trust; I shall not be afraid (Ps. 56:4).

Then they believed His words; they sang His praise (Ps. 106:12).

God's character. Since most of these examples represent praise from the Psalms, this list is not exhaustive. Obviously, every characteristic of God deserves praise.

- *Righteousness (Ps. 7:17)*
- *Everlasting loving-kindness (Ezra 3:11; 2 Chron. 5:13; 20:21; Ps. 63:3; 117:2)*

- *Power (Ps. 21:13)*
- *Goodness (Ezra 3:11; Ps. 135:3)*
- *Excellent greatness (Ps. 48:1; 66:3-4; 96:4; 145:3)*
- *Glory (Eph. 1:6, 12, 14)*

The list could be largely expanded to include such qualities as His mercy, grace, patience, holiness, and many others.

God's conduct. Praise proves appropriate for all that God does. Several areas that Scripture particularly focuses on include:

- *Help/deliverance (Ps. 145:4; Jer. 20:13)*
- *Works (Ps. 145:4; 150:2; Isa. 12:5)*
- *Healing (Luke 18:43)*
- *Eternal dominion (Dan. 4:34)*

Praise Instruments

Music seems to be the major way to praise God, particularly when His people have gathered for corporate worship. A survey of the Old Testament points out that praise came from a wide assortment of sources—from a 4,000-piece praise orchestra (1 Chron. 23:5) to a 10-string harp (Ps. 33:2). Specific instruments included:

- *Cymbals (Ezra 3:10; Ps. 150:5)*
- *Lyre (Ps. 43:4; 71:22; 98:5; 147:7; 149:3; 150:3)*
- *Harp (Ps. 71:22; 150:3)*
- *Timbrel (Ps. 149:3; 150:4)*
- *Trumpet (Ezra 3:10; Ps. 150:3)*
- *Pipe (Ps. 150:4)*
- *Stringed instruments (Ps. 150:4)*

It's safe to say that any instrument capable of playing music may be used to praise God and draw attention to Him.

Of course, singing is always in. The first recorded praise song came from Moses (Ex. 15:1-18), who wrote to celebrate God's victory over Pharaoh and Israel's liberation from the Egyptians. "The Lord is my strength and song, and He has become my salvation; this is my God, and I will praise Him, my father's God, and I will extol Him" (v. 2).

Deborah and Barak co-wrote a hymn of celebration to give God all the glory for their victory over the Canaanites (Jud. 5:2-31). The psalmist commended song as a means of praise when he wrote, "I will praise the name of God with song, and shall magnify Him with thanksgiving" (Ps. 69:30; see also 2 Sam. 22:50; 1 Chron. 16:9; Ps. 9:11).

Famous Praise Gatherings

Leah and Jacob praised God for the birth of Judah, whose name in Hebrew signifies "praise" (Gen. 29:35). The nation Israel gave a praise offering to God as a part of tabernacle worship (Lev. 19:24). Moses told the Israelites, "[God] is your praise" (Deut. 10:21). The Levites and priests praised God daily for seven days during the Feast of Unleavened Bread (2 Chron. 30:21).

Solomon praised God for His everlasting loving-kindness during the dedication of the temple (2 Chron. 5:13). Four centuries later Ezra praised the Lord for the rebuilt temple (Ezra 3:10-11). Nehemiah (Neh. 12:46) and Daniel (Dan. 2:23) both praised God for what He had done on their behalf.

The birth of Jesus prompted tremendous praise, first from the angels (Luke 2:13) and then from the shepherds (v. 20).

Perhaps the most unusual praise time, but also the most appropriate, occurred in a prison experience.

And the crowd rose up together against them [Paul and Silas], and the chief magistrates tore their robes off them, and proceeded to order them to be beaten with rods. And ... they threw them into prison, commanding the jailer to guard them securely; and he, having received such a command, threw them into the inner prison, and fastened their feet in the stocks. But about midnight Paul and Silas were praying and singing hymns of praise to God, and the prisoners were listening to them (Acts 16:22-25).

In times of need or plenty, when life is on the mountaintop

or in the dark valley, by yourself or with God's people, with or without music, praise can appropriately be given to God. Even if it comes out as simple as "Praise the Lord" (Ps. 104:35; 105:45; 106:1).

A New Song

One of the great scriptural themes focuses on the new song sung by those who have put their faith in God for eternal life. That song comes from God (Ps. 40:3), is encouraged by the psalmists (33:3; 96:1; 98:1; 149:1), and becomes the righteous response of the redeemed (144:9-10).

It's a song that can be sung by new creations in Christ (2 Cor. 5:17) who now sing in a new way. It's new in that the song was not sung by us before salvation; thus it is new in time and content.

The new song demonstrates and certifies a new relationship with God. It's a fresh song that proves uncommon to mankind in general.

The Christmas carol "Joy to the World" came from the pen of Isaac Watts who was touched by the words of Psalm 98. Look there with me a moment as I point out the features of this prototype praise song.

1. It's to be sung to the Lord (v. 1)
2. It's sung about His great deeds (vv. 1-3)
3. It's rendered for the purpose of praise (v. 4)
4. It focuses on the saviourship of God (vv. 2-3)
5. It focuses on the kingship of God (vv. 4-6)
6. It focuses on the judgeship of God (vv. 7-9)

The magnum opus, however, will be sung by the combined voice of heaven's inhabitants.

And when He had taken the book, the four living creatures and the twenty-four elders fell down before the Lamb, having each one harp, and golden bowls full of incense, which are the prayers of the saints. And they sang a new song, saying, "Worthy art Thou to take the book, and to break its seals; for Thou wast slain, and didst purchase for God with Thy blood men from every tribe and tongue and people and nation. And Thou hast made them to be a kingdom and priests to our God; and they will reign upon the earth."

And I looked, and I heard the voice of many angels around the throne and the living creatures and the elders; and the number of them was myriads of myriads, and thousands of thousands, saying with a loud voice, "Worthy is the Lamb that was slain to receive power and riches and wisdom and might and honor and glory and blessing."

And every created thing which is in heaven and on the earth and under the earth and on the sea, and all things in them, I heard saying, "To Him who sits on the throne, and to the Lamb, be blessing and honor and glory and dominion forever and ever."

And the four living creatures kept saying "Amen." And the elders fell down and worshiped (Rev. 5:8-14).

Scripture also teaches that God's Spirit orchestrates praise.

And do not get drunk with wine, for that is dissipation, but be filled with the Spirit, speaking to one another in psalms and hymns and spiritual songs, singing and making melody with your heart to the Lord; always giving thanks for all things in the name of our Lord Jesus Christ to God, even the Father (Eph. 5:18-20).

Praise then marks the person who yields to God's Spirit. What could be more appropriate in a spiritual sense than God's Spirit living in God's people directing praise to God the Father and God the Son in heaven?

No wonder "The Doxology" has long been enthusiastically sung by God's people. If you are as overwhelmed by this theme as I am, you might want to sing now, just as I did when I penned this chapter:

Praise God, from whom all blessings flow;
Praise Him all creatures here below;
Praise Him above, ye heavenly hosts
Praise Father, Son, and Holy Ghost.

Praise Practitioners

It's amazing to read what the Bible says about praise. To sum it up, all things are to the praise of God. The creatures on earth praise (Ps. 69:34; 89:5; 148:1) as do the heavens (148:3). Both angels (Job 38:7, KJV; Ps. 148:2) and humans praise God. In case anyone feels left out, the Psalms end with this invitation: "Let everything that has breath praise the Lord. Praise the Lord!" (Ps. 150:6)

Praise marked Israel's worship in the nation's godly times, for we read: "And Hezekiah appointed the divisions of the priests and the Levites by their divisions, each according to his service, both the priests and the Levites, for burnt offerings and for peace offerings, to minister and to give thanks and to praise in the gates of the camp of the Lord" (2 Chron. 31:2).

Praise likewise highlighted the early church's experience: "And all those who believed were together . . . praising God, and having favor with all people. And the Lord was adding to their number day by day those who were being saved" (Acts 2:44, 47).

Praise knew nothing about the separation of church and state. From the lips of Babylon's King Nebuchadnezzar (Dan. 4:34) and from the mouth of the priest Zacharias (Luke 1:64) flowed praise.

Praise equally graced the lips of Christ who was sinless (Matt. 11:25) and Achan who would shortly die for his transgression (Josh. 7:19-20).

Praise is for everyone and everything. "For it is written: 'As I live, says the Lord, every knee shall bow to Me, and every tongue shall give praise to God' " (Rom. 14:11; see also Isa. 45:23).

Praise Companions
Blessing God and thanking God often accompany praise in Scripture. Indeed, these three form an inseparable trio (see also Ps. 34:1; 66:8; 68:26; 115:18).

Enter His gates with thanksgiving, and His courts with praise. Give thanks to Him; bless His name (Ps. 100:4).

Everyone knows David's famous self-invitation to praise. It makes a great praise chorus.

Bless the Lord, O my soul; and all that is within me, bless His holy name (Ps. 103:1).

Praise and thanksgiving frequently appear in tandem (see also Ps. 18:49; 30:4; 35:18; 69:30).

It is good to give thanks to the Lord, and to sing praises to Thy name, O Most High (Ps. 92:1).

Sing to the Lord with thanksgiving; sing praises to our God on the lyre (Ps. 147:7).

The New Testament features thanksgiving just as prominently as the Old.

In everything give thanks; for this is God's will for you in Christ Jesus (1 Thes. 5:18).

Through Him then, let us continually offer up a sacrifice of praise to God, that is, the fruit of lips that give thanks to His name (Heb. 13:15).

Praise Tips
1. Obey the strong, scriptural call to praise God.

Sing praises to God, sing praises; sing praises to our King, sing praises. For God is the King of all the earth; sing praises with a skillful psalm (Ps. 47:6-7).

Shout joyfully to God, all the earth; sing the glory of His name; make His praise glorious. Say to God, "How awesome are Thy works! Because of the greatness of Thy power Thine enemies will give feigned obedience to Thee; all the earth will worship Thee, and will sing praises to Thee; they will sing praises to Thy name" (Ps. 66:1-4).

2. Look at Psalms 145–150 for worshipful patterns of praise.
3. Praise God every day (Ps. 145:2).
4. Praise God many times daily (Ps. 119:164).
5. Praise God from sunup to sundown (Ps. 71:8).

Praise the Lord! Praise, O servants of the Lord. Praise the name of the Lord. Blessed be the name of the Lord from this time forth and forever. From the rising of the sun to its setting the name of the Lord is to be praised (Ps. 113:1-3).

6. Praise God until death and then forever.

I will sing to the Lord as long as I live; I will sing praise to my God while I have my being (Ps. 104:33).

I will extol Thee, my God, O King; and I will bless Thy name forever and ever (Ps. 145:1).

7. Conduct yourself with praise, for such behavior is becoming to a righteous person at all times.

Sing for joy in the Lord, O you righteous ones; praise is becoming to the upright (Ps. 33:1).

Praise the Lord! For it is good to sing praises to our God;

for it is pleasant and praise is becoming (Ps. 147:1).

8. Make praise a continual habit of your life.

I will bless the Lord at all times; His praise will continually be in my mouth (Ps. 34:1).

9. Think on things that are worthy of praise.

Finally, brethren, whatever is true, whatever is honorable, whatever is right, whatever is pure, whatever is lovely, whatever is of good repute, if there is any excellence and if anything worthy of praise, let your mind continually dwell on these things (Phil. 4:8).

10. Join the throngs in heaven and on earth who find great joy in praising God. Pray that God will fill you with praise.

O Lord, open my lips, that my mouth may declare Thy praise (Ps. 51:15).

A Final Note
Augustine wrote that the Christian should be "an Alleluia" from head to foot. A master of music illustrates this point.

Joseph Haydn was present at the Vienna Music Hall where his oratorio *The Creation* was being performed. Weakened by age, the great composer was confined to a wheelchair. As the majestic work moved along, the audience was caught up with tremendous emotion. When the passage, "And there was light!" was reached, the chorus and orchestra burst forth in such power that the crowd could no longer restrain its enthusiasm. The grandeur of the music and the presence of the composer himself brought the vast assembly to its feet in spontaneous applause. Haydn struggled to get out of his wheelchair. Finally up, he motioned for silence. The enraptured crowd heard him call out with what strength he could muster, hand pointed toward heaven, "No, no, not from me, but from thence comes all!" Having given the glory and praise to the Creator, he fell back into his chair exhausted.

AMEN!

I will sacrifice a freewill offering to you;
I will praise Your name, O Lord,
for it is good.
Psalm 54:6 (NIV)

7
GIVING TO GOD

A young man came out of the Ozark Mountains in his early manhood with the firm purpose of making a fortune. Gold became his god, and putting it first, he won it. He came to be worth millions. Then the crash came, and he was reduced to utter poverty. His reason tottered and fell along with his fortune.

A mere beggar, he took to the road where one day a policeman found him on Eads Bridge gazing down into the waters of the Mississippi and ordered him to move on. "Let me alone," the despondent man answered. "I am trying to think. There is something that is better than gold, but I have forgotten what it is." They placed him in an institution for the insane. They knew that a man who could forget *that* was not himself.[1]

As the twentieth century draws to a close, it seems that we have revisited the days when people worship at the shrine of materialism. Our society trusts money to do for them what

God has promised to do, in spite of the little motto printed on our coins and bills, "In God We Trust."

I recently read that the average giving among Christians in America is only 2.5 percent of their adjusted gross income.[2] That's a far cry from the 23⅓ percent the Old Testament required (Lev. 27:30; Deut. 12:10-11; 14:28). While I do not believe the New Testament teaches tithing as a legal obligation, the current trend falls enormously below even 10 percent. Therefore, we need to be reminded of what God's Word teaches, and then reorient our budgets to reflect a true worship of God, not of materialism.

Spiritual intimacy demands that we revive our giving to God and reduce our search for the "good life." Can you imagine what would happen if every Christian gave just 9 percent as a "firstfruits" offering? (Prov. 3:9) It would be like the days of Moses (Ex. 36:1-7) and David (1 Chron. 29:1-20). People brought so much back then that they had an abundance.

In order to stimulate us all to the appropriate level of blessing (Acts 20:35), our discussion first centers on the greatest message ever written on giving. Then we'll distill some biblical principles on which godly giving can be based. The ABCs of "grace giving" will top off our thoughts on giving as a means of drawing closer to God.

Paul on Giving

Hard times had struck the church in Jerusalem. It became fitting for the church elsewhere to take up a collection for these distressed brethren in the faith. While on his third missionary journey (Acts 18:23–21:16), Paul carried Jerusalem's cause to the church in Macedonia and Achaia (modern-day Greece) with the intention of taking their offering to Jerusalem himself (Rom. 15:25-26). In preparation for his upcoming visit, Paul included a major exhortation on giving to the church in Corinth.

He had written briefly about giving once before (1 Cor.

16:1-4); now he writes in earnest. The first major thought focuses on the northern churches in Macedonia — Thessalonica and Philippi (2 Cor. 8:1-5). He commends them as an example of "grace giving" because although they possessed little, they gave much. Three major ideas stand out:

1. Even though they were poor, they gave above and beyond the call of duty (vv. 2-3).
2. They did not give because they felt pressured, but because they wanted to (v. 3).
3. They gave according to God's will, not their own (v. 5).

Paul then turns his attention to the Corinthians themselves who had pledged much but given little (vv. 6-15). Central to this exhortation, Paul focuses on the Lord Jesus Christ — and how He gave at Calvary — as a model for the Corinthians:

For you know the grace of our Lord Jesus Christ, that though He was rich, yet for your sake He became poor, that you through His poverty might become rich (2 Cor. 8:9).

It seems as though the Corinthians wished to wait longer because the time was not right; prosperous times hadn't arrived. So, Paul urges them to give now out of their current riches (8:10-12); and he appeals to the truth that God gives us an abundance as a means to help those who do not have enough, even for the basics (vv. 13-15).

Paul also admonishes them to fulfill their promise to God. He assures them that responsible leaders will render accountable stewardship to the funds collected (vv. 16-24). Even more, their giving "example" should be bountiful and not minimized by a spirit of covetousness (9:1-5).

Paul closes with instructions on "grace giving" (9:6-15). He gives the Corinthian Christians four basics:

1. What you plant will determine what you harvest (v. 6).
2. God desires giving with a selfless attitude (v. 7).
3. God will provide the financial seed, if it is to be sown in

the cause of righteousness (vv. 8-11).

4. Right giving leads to right worship of God (vv. 12-15).

And my God shall supply all your needs according to His riches in glory in Christ Jesus (Phil. 4:19).

Principles for Giving

Someone has noted, "God is not poor; neither are Christians broke." Yet at times it seems that way when we look at the finances of many local churches. Why? I believe it results from a combination of factors.

First, many pastors do not teach and practice "grace giving" in their churches. Consequently, Christians do not know about and cannot give according to grace. Third, Christians who *do* know scriptural standards for giving ignore them, choosing instead to indulge themselves rather than to sacrificially invest in the eternal matters of God's kingdom.

Following are the most basic principles presented in Scripture designed to govern the giving patterns of every Christian:

1. *Recognize that* all *we have is a gift from God* (Ex. 19:5; Ps. 50:10-12; 1 Tim. 6:7). From a communistic viewpoint, the state owns it all. In capitalism, the individual possesses all; but with Christianity, everything belongs to God because He created it (John 1:3).

Job exemplifies the principle, not so much in the good times, but rather at their loss.

And he said, "Naked I came from my mother's womb, and naked I shall return there. The Lord gave and the Lord has taken away. Blessed be the name of the Lord" (Job 1:21).

2. *Giving should be planned and regular as a part of your personal worship* (1 Cor. 16:2). Three elements stand out. First, giving should be done with planned regularity—here Paul teaches to do it weekly on the Lord's Day. Next it is to

be personal—"each one of you." There are to be no exemptions. Third, give at whatever level God has given to you during that period. So the only possible reason for not giving is that you received nothing. Even then, a person could normally reach back to times when he or she received an overabundance.

3. *Give freely through a "purposed heart"* (2 Cor. 8:3; 9:7). Three types of giving have been identified over the years: the "flint" giver who must be hammered; the "sponge" giver who must be squeezed; and the "honeycomb" giver who overflows. What kind are you?

Jesus first articulated this principle to the disciples as they were about to go out in ministry. "Freely you received, freely give" (Matt. 10:8). The point is this—grace received is to be grace given.

4. *Giving involves a commitment to the Lord and trust in godly leaders* (2 Cor. 8:5). The Macedonians gave first to the Lord by way of a commitment and then executed the plan by actually entrusting the money to Paul and other spiritual leaders. They did this in the same way that the church of Jerusalem laid their gifts at the feet of the apostles (Acts 4:35).

Look at it this way. All of your assets belong to God, who by His will desires you to give for the establishment and extension of His church worldwide. Not only do your resources belong to God, but they are to be received and expended by godly leaders, not you. So it becomes critical that you first find godly leaders who are committed to God's will and then give in abundance.

5. *Giving is not optional* (2 Cor. 8:12). Many people believe that they can give nonmonetary gifts in lieu of money, or that they can wait until their personal plans are fulfilled and then give abundantly. God soundly rebukes this sort of thinking in Haggai 1:5-11. The Jews worked hard but accumulated little, because building their own homes had higher priority than investing in God's kingdom.

Paul's point is unmistakable—give out of what you have. Don't postpone your giving; for to do so is to tell God that He is less than first in your life.

6. *"Liberality" best describes New Testament giving* (1 Cor. 16:2; 2 Cor. 8:2-3; 9:11-13). In your giving, does God get the first and the best or the last and the least? How you give reflects accurately what you think of God and the apple of His eye—the church. The percentage given by each believer will be different with the freedom of grace, but the level should always be sacrificial. Giving should be done with David's heart: "I will not offer burnt offerings to the Lord my God which cost me nothing" (2 Sam. 24:24; 1 Chron. 21:24).

7. *Giving will be reviewed at the Judgment Seat of Christ* (2 Cor. 5:10). Present needs should drive our giving, but so should our future appointment to stand before Christ. Salvation doesn't enter into the issue here, but rewards and loss in eternity, based on how we conducted our Christian life on earth, does (see 1 Cor. 3:15).

Whether God's Spirit has enabled you with the special gift of giving (Rom. 12:8) or you give as a part of your regular Christian duty, there will be a day of accountability.

8. *Giving will bring great blessing to the giver* (Acts 20:35).

Not only did Jesus and Paul preach this wonderful truth, but the Philippian church experienced the blessing. After receiving a generous gift, Paul writes to remind them that a part of his joy results from the blessing they received in giving. "Not that I seek the gift itself, but I seek for the profit which increases to your account" (Phil. 4:17).

In some senses, giving becomes the means to gigantic spiritual blessing. God is pleased or blessed with sacrifice (Heb. 13:16). The giver is blessed and the work of God is blessed in that it is enjoying advances continually.

Practice of Giving
So far we've looked at the most influential scriptural text on giving (2 Cor. 8–9) and have surveyed the basics of giving.

Now, let's turn all of this knowledge into a practical plan that will allow you to be a doer of the Word, not a mere hearer (James 1:22).

First, acknowledge that God really does own all of your assets by taking an inventory of them. Then prayerfully thank Him for loaning them to you.

Think about how you handle other people's property when it is in your possession—with care and a plan to return it in as good or better condition than received. This attitude should also prevail toward God.

A missionary in India once visited a Hindu temple which had been elaborately adorned with precious metals. He asked a nearby worshiper, "How much did you pay for this?" "Money?" was the reply. "We never count the cost when it is for our gods." And how much more for us who have been redeemed by Christ and worship the true God.

Second, personally accept your spiritual responsibility as a steward of God's possessions. The Jews in Malachi's day failed to take this truth seriously and received biting indictments from God. They had given God second best (Mal. 1:7-9). Even worse, they had robbed God by spending on themselves rather than giving as God instructed (3:8-10).

You might want to ask these questions about both your giving and personal spending:

1. Will this build Christ's church?
2. Will this advance God's kingdom?
3. Will this make an eternal impact?
4. Will this please and glorify God?
5. Will this be in God's will?

Third, pray for God's wisdom and grace in your disbursement of His riches. "But if any of you lacks wisdom, let him ask of God, who gives to all men generously and without reproach, and it will be given to him" (James 1:5).

When we first became Christians, my wife "B" and I asked this question: "Do we give from the gross or the net?" Put another way: "Do we give before or after taxes?" Wisdom directed that we give to God as He gave to us.

What does this mean practically? Initially, it meant spending according to a plan that put God first. As we reduced our expenditures, that allowed us the freedom to make our first disbursement the money we gave to God.

Then we decided to base our giving on what God gave us before such expenditures as taxes or Social Security. We also decided that what we gave on the Lord's Day didn't need to be our maximum but our minimum. That's been our habit for twenty years now and I joyfully commend it to you.

Fourth, evaluate your giving to the Lord and ask yourself if God would classify your giving as gracious, generous, and/or liberal. The real issue in deciding this is not how much you give, but rather, how much you have left after giving.

Let me illustrate with a day in Jesus' ministry:

And He looked up and saw the rich putting their gifts into the treasury. And He saw a certain poor widow putting in two small copper coins. And He said, "Truly I say to you this poor widow put in more than all of them; for they all out of their surplus put into the offering; but she out of her poverty put in all she had to live on" (Luke 21:1-4).

Look again at Christ's comment on her giving, "Truly I say to you, this poor widow put in more than all of them." What did He mean? Four lessons rivet themselves to our souls if we're serious about giving:

1. It was not her social prominence that drew Christ's pleasure—for she was a widow.
2. Her wealth didn't please Him—for she was poor.
3. The amount of her contribution didn't solicit Christ's comments—for the two mites constituted far less than one day's wage.
4. Christ *did* find pleasure in what she had left over after she gave and in what she did without to give—for she put in all that she had to live on.

It could be that God wants you to be like R.G. LeTourneau who practiced "reverse tithing." He gave 90 percent and kept the other 10.

Fifth, give bountifully to your local church first before you give elsewhere. Both the Bible and logic demand that our primary giving go to the place where we're fed, loved, cared for, accountable, and where we have spiritual family plus personal involvement. "And let the one who is taught the Word share all good things with him who teaches" (Gal. 6:6).

Sixth, ask God to make "grace giving" a joyous, spiritual habit in your life. Then apply the truths, the principles, and the practices we have just discussed.

Sacrificial Giving

After I had preached a message on giving, my secretary asked, "What is sacrificial giving and how do you know if you're giving at that level?" While I wasn't then and still am not sure of a scientifically precise answer, I am convinced that it involves attitude and action rather than an absolute amount. So my response to Kim sounded something like, "Sacrificial giving is postponing or foregoing an earthly pleasure to provide for the kingdom's advancement." If the attitude and actions are right, then the amount will surely please God.

John Wanamaker, a wealthy nineteenth-century Philadelphia merchant, once made a trip to China to determine how well the money he had given to missions was being used. He came upon an old man plowing with a crude apparatus drawn by an ox and a young man. Asking for an explanation, Wanamaker was told that his chapel needed a spire to be visible for miles around. The church members prayed, but the money given was still not enough. Then a son said to his father, "Let us sell one of the oxen and I will take the yoke of the ox we sell."

Wanamaker then prayed, "Lord, let me be hitched to a plow, so that I may know the joy of sacrificial giving."

O God, Thou art my God; I shall seek Thee
earnestly; my soul thirsts for Thee, my flesh
yearns for Thee, in a dry and weary land
where there is no water.
Psalm 63:1

8
PURSUING GOD

After I preached one Sunday with some strong warnings about psychology, a young "psych" major asked for an appointment to discuss my views. His question focused on the biblical basis for my comments.

I had not intended to dismiss the discipline as utterly worthless or leave the impression that anyone who studied psychology had compromised his faith. However, he did catch my less-than-enthusiastic support for the discipline of psychology in general and more pointedly, for its growing emphasis in Christian circles to the point of relegating God's Word to a secondary role.

Later, over breakfast, I explained to him that psychology as a modern discipline rested on godless assumptions and had been promoted mainly by intellectuals who deny God.[1] Thus, they spawned an approach to life that is man-centered, not God-centered. That clearly contradicts the major emphasis of Scripture. My point simply stated is this: Theology might lead to some valid "psychological" conclusions but psychology will never lead a person to God.

Scripture mandates that godliness become the Christian's quest. In other words, life must be God-centered. "Therefore you are to be perfect, as your Heavenly Father is perfect" (Matt. 5:48).

Both Paul (1 Tim. 4:7; 6:6) and Peter (2 Peter 1:3, 6) commend godliness as the believer's worthiest aim. As physical children become "chips off the old block," so spiritual children should seek to perfect in themselves the image in whose likeness they were created. Christianity demands this; psychology as a modern discipline doesn't even encourage it.

Seeking God

Both theology and psychology explore the inner man. They look beyond the physical. But Paul distinguishes between the temporal and the eternal, while psychology does not.

Therefore we do not lose heart, but though our outer man is decaying, yet our inner man is being renewed day by day (2 Cor. 4:16).

Then the apostle indicates that through prayer and the power of God's Spirit, our "inner man" can be strengthened. That's the unique Christian approach to life on this side of heaven.

That He would grant you, according to the riches of His glory, to be strengthened with power through His Spirit in the inner man (Eph. 3:16).

We popularly refer to this truth through the vivid pen of Isaiah:

He gives strength to the weary, and to him who lacks might He increases power. Though youths grow weary and tired, and vigorous young men stumble badly, yet those who wait for the Lord will gain new strength; they will mount up with wings like eagles, they will run and not get tired, they will walk and not get weary (Isa. 40:29-31).

Thus as Christians, Scripture exhorts us to be:
1. Conformed to the image of Christ (Rom. 8:29; Col. 3:10)
2. Transformed into God's glory (2 Cor. 3:18)
3. Imitators of God (1 Cor. 4:16-17; 11:1; Eph. 5:1)
4. Christlike because we are Christians (Acts 11:26; 1 Peter 4:16)
5. Holy Spiritlike (1 Cor. 2:14-15; Gal. 5:22-23; Rom. 8:6-9)
6. Godlike or godly (2 Tim. 3:12; Titus 2:12)

To do this we must seek God as a first priority, not man nor the things of this earth. Moses preached this (Deut. 12:5), as did David (1 Chron. 16:10-11; 22:19). The most memorable exhortation came from Jesus: "But seek first His kingdom and His righteousness; and all these things shall be added to you" (Matt. 6:33).

God makes some tremendous promises to those who seek Him. He gives:
1. Protection............Ps. 9:10
2. Provision ....Ps. 34:10
3. Blessing ....Ps. 119:2
4. Goodness ....Lam. 3:25
5. Reward ....Heb. 11:6

How does this all work out in life? A literary snapshot in the life of Justin Martyr (A.D. 100–165) illustrates the ultimate and intimate Christian seeker.

Around 165, Justin and six other Christians were arrested for their faith and brought to trial before Rusticus, the Roman prefect.

Rusticus asked him, "Are you a Christian?"

"Yes," Justin answered. "I am."

"Then, let's come to the matter at hand," Rusticus said. "Sacrifice to the gods."

"No one who is rightly minded turns from true belief to false."

"If you do not obey," the prefect said, "you'll be punished without mercy."

"If we are punished for the sake of our Lord Jesus Christ," Justin said, "we hope to be saved, for this shall be our salvation and confidence before the terrible Judgment Seat of our Saviour and Lord who shall judge the world."

The other believers agreed: "Do what you will," they said. "We are Christians, and we do not sacrifice to idols."

Immediately the sentence fell. All seven were taken from the court and beheaded.[2]

Following Christ

Those who seek will also follow. Jesus came to seek and save those who needed eternal life (Luke 19:10). When He found them, He beckoned them to "Follow Me!"

On at least eight distinct occasions Jesus issued forth His famous call (see also John 12:26).

1. Andrew and Simon Peter .... Matt. 4:18-19
2. John and James .... Matt. 4:20-21
3. Unidentified disciples................... Matt. 8:22
4. Matthew .... Matt. 9:9
5. The Twelve .... Matt. 16:24
6. Rich young ruler .... Matt. 19:21
7. Philip ....John 1:43
8. Simon Peter .... John 21:19, 22

The sheep of Christ's flock characteristically follow the Shepherd. "My sheep hear My voice, and I know them, and they follow Me" (John 10:27).

This simple command reached new levels of impact for me as I read a letter from a man serving time in a federal penitentiary on drug charges. This former businessman gloriously received Christ as his "Lord and Saviour" in prison. While reading my previous book *Unmasking Satan*, he came to a chapter that applied to his married life and wrote to me with a very important question. Its essence was, "How do I follow Jesus in this situation?"

What does a husband and the Bible say to a wife who is committed to waiting? Has my incarceration or rather should my incarceration relieve her of her marital responsibility? In other words, should she suffer while I'm locked up? ... What does an incarcerated man say to his wife about loneliness, sex, companionship, and temptation? Are our wives commanded by the Bible to hold on and wait for their husbands? Or out of love and concern for our wives should we divorce them and tell them to find another man for companionship?

This man fervently desired to follow Christ. Both he and his wife just wanted to know what Jesus said so that they could obey. In case you're wondering how I responded, it went something like this — "Stay married, stay pure, and seek God for the patience and strength to do the humanly impossible."

Imitating the Holy Spirit
I found it interesting to discover in Scripture that when God commanded us to embrace a certain quality, at times He said "Be like Me!" We are to be pure, like God (1 John 3:3). Our love should be like God's love (1 John 4:7-17; Eph. 5:2). Since God is holy, we are to be holy also (Lev. 19:2; 1 Peter 1:14-16).

The ultimate test of a vegetable garden or orchard is the produce or fruit which it bears. Likewise, Christian growth is not measured by our size or by how long we have been growing but rather by the quality of fruit manifest in our lives.

God gave us His Spirit as the proper spiritual model so that the fruit harvested in our lives would mark us out as genuine. The degree of Spiritlike fruit growing on the limbs of our lives unmistakably gauges just how intimate we are with God.

Galatians 5:22-23 pictures the Spirit-produced fruit that evidences a truly healthy Christian:

But the fruit of the Spirit is love, joy, peace, patience, kindness, goodness, faithfulness, gentleness, self-control; against such things there is no law.

Have someone you trust and respect climb through your life and see what kind of fruit they can discover. Will it match up with Holy Spirit-produced fruit like this?

1. *Love.* A sacrificial commitment to the welfare of another person regardless of that person's response or what he or she might give to me in return.
2. *Joy.* A deep, abiding inner thankfulness to God for His goodness that is not interrupted when less desirable life circumstances intrude.
3. *Peace.* Heartfelt tranquility and trust during the storms of life that are anchored in the overwhelming consciousness that I am in the hand of God.
4. *Patience.* A quality of self-restraint which does not hastily retaliate in the face of provoking situations.
5. *Kindness.* A sensitive awareness and willingness to seek out ways in which to serve others.
6. *Goodness.* An unswerving capacity to deal with people rightly in the best interest of God even when correction is required.
7. *Faithfulness.* An inner unyieldingness that results in remaining true to my spiritual convictions and commitments.
8. *Gentleness.* Controlled strength that is dispensed from a humble heart.
9. *Self-control.* An inward, personal mastery that submits my desires to the greater cause of God's will.

We can imitate God's Holy Spirit with His help and power.

Learning from the Master

Disciples and discipleship dominate the pages of the Gospels and Acts, with over 250 mentions. The words refer to a learner/mentor relationship. To become a Christian is to become a learner who sits at the feet of a newfound master— Jesus Christ. "Take My yoke and learn from Me" has become one of the most memorable of Christ's invitations to eternal life (Matt. 11:29).

In the Book of Acts, where Luke focuses on believers and their activities, every time the concept appears, with one exception (29 times), it refers to a Christian. There is no distinction between being a believer now and a disciple later. The whole church is referred to as disciples (Acts 6:2, 7; 15:10; 18:23). Acts 26:28 compared with Acts 11:26 equates being a Christian with being a disciple (see also 9:26; 20:30).

One becomes a disciple by responding to God's gospel of grace (14:21; 18:27). There are no instances of a "non-disciple" believer. One writer summarizes his conclusions about the learner/master relationship with Jesus in an unforgettable way.

The disciple of Jesus is not the deluxe or heavy-duty model of the Christian—specially padded, textured, streamlined and empowered for the fast lane on the straight and narrow way. He stands on the pages of the New Testament as the first level of basic transportation in the kingdom of God.[3]

I recently read a story that riveted itself to my mind. As you read it, remember that Communism bears no eternal value, while Christianity remains humanity's only forever hope.

In the late 1940s Whittaker Chambers was called to witness before a New York Grand Jury against Alger Hiss, one of our high government officials. Chambers, a one-time Communist, accused Hiss of trying to transmit confiden-

tial government documents to the Soviet Union through him. When asked what it means to be a Communist by one of the jurors, Chambers struggled to provide a clear answer. Finally he told them that when he was a Communist, he had three heroes.

His first hero was a Pole, a political prisoner in Warsaw. While there, he insisted on cleaning the latrines of the other prisoners because he felt that the most devoted member of any community should take upon himself the lowliest tasks as an example to those who were less devoted. "That," said Chambers, "is one thing it means to be a Communist."

His second hero was a German Jew who was captured and court-martialed during a revolution in Bavaria. When told that he was now under the sentence of death he replied, "We Communists are always under the sentence of death." "That," said Chambers, "is another thing it means to be a Communist."

His third hero was a Russian exiled to a Siberian prison camp where political prisoners were flogged. He sought some means of protesting that inhumane persecution. Finally in desperation he drenched himself in kerosene, set himself on fire, and burned himself to death as a protest against what he considered a great indignity. "That," repeated Chambers, "is also what it means to be a Communist."[4]

Pursuing God is not learning about a system like Communism, but rather learning from a person—Christ. As we learn, we will become like Him (Luke 6:40).

Running the Race

The summer of 1984 proved unique to the city of Los Angeles, for its proud citizens played host to the Olympic games. As part of the pins and paraphernalia, I heard about an Olympic banner which read, *"Citius, Altius, Fortius."* It's the Latin motto for the Olympics which means "swifter, higher, stronger."

Paul had the similar Isthmian games of ancient Greece in mind when he wrote:

Do you not know that those who run in a race all run, but only one receives the prize? Run in such a way that you may win. And everyone who competes in the games exercises self-control in all things. They then do it to receive a perishable wreath, but we an imperishable. Therefore I run in such a way, as not without aim; I box in such a way, as not beating the air; but I buffet my body and make it my slave, lest possibly, after I have preached to others, I myself should be disqualified (1 Cor. 9:24-27; see also Phil. 3:12-14).

The place for the race was called the stadium because its course was a stadium, or 600 Greek feet, in length. The goal rested at the opposite end from the starting point. There stood the judge with the prize in his hand. In Paul's day, the crown was made of wilted celery stalks.[5]

For the apostle, his heavenly crown of righteousness (2 Tim. 4:8), of unfading glory (1 Peter 5:4), of eternal life (James 1:12; Rev. 2:10), and with imperishable quality (1 Cor. 9:25), made the effort of running the Christian life worth it all. He pressed with all of his might toward the goal of heaven and glory for the prize of eternal life. No wonder he could proclaim victory from the Mamertine Prison in Rome even with the sentence of death imminent. "I have fought the good fight, I have finished the course, I have kept the faith" (2 Tim. 4:7).

As Paul pressed, so are we to press. We are to pursue with every ounce of energy these Christian qualities:

1. Hospitality .... Rom. 12:13
2. Godliness .... 1 Tim. 6:11
3. Goodness .... 1 Thes. 5:15

4. Peace....................1 Peter 3:11; Rom. 14:19;
   2 Tim. 2:22; Heb. 12:14
5. Love ....1 Cor. 14:1; 1 Tim. 6:11;
   2 Tim. 2:22
6. Righteousness ....1 Tim. 6:11; 2 Tim. 2:22
7. Faith ....1 Tim. 6:11; 2 Tim. 2:22
8. Perseverance ....1 Tim. 6:11
9. Gentleness ....1 Tim. 6:11

The writer of Hebrews gives us one final tip on our running style. It will equip us for a swifter, higher, and stronger race.

Therefore, since we have so great a cloud of witnesses surrounding us, let us also lay aside every encumbrance, and the sin which so easily entangles us, and let us run with endurance the race that is set before us, fixing our eyes on Jesus, the author and perfecter of faith, who for the joy set before Him endured the cross, despising the shame, and has sat down at the right hand of the throne of God (Heb. 12:1-2).

Battling the Enemy

Pursuing God also involves traveling through enemy territory, including skirmishes with Satan and his army of hell. The Christian dare not be without his armor.

Therefore, take up the full armor of God, that you may be able to resist in the evil day, and having done everything, to stand firm. Stand firm therefore, having girded your loins with truth, and having put on the breastplate of righteousness, and having shod your feet with the preparation of the Gospel of peace; in addition to all, taking up the shield of faith with which you will be able to extinguish all the flaming missiles of the evil one. And take the helmet of salvation, and the sword of the Spirit, which is the word of God (Eph. 6:13-17).

Having been a Naval officer for over five years, including one year of "shore duty" in Vietnam, I retain a rather vivid image of battlefield reality. However, it reached a new level recently when I invited veteran Christian and Missionary Alliance missionary Herb Clingen into my classroom to share his life and ministry with the moldable young men at The Master's Seminary.

Herb recounted the days that he and his family had been incarcerated by the Japanese in the Philippines during World War II. After treatment became more brutal and just when they and hundreds of others were about to be executed, American army troops pulled off a daring rescue. All of the missionaries were liberated.

Over forty years had passed since that February 24, 1945 release. In 1989, Herb and his wife Ruth met for the first time with the officer who engineered their rescue decades earlier. Herb was able to share that just as this officer had liberated them from the Japanese, they wanted in turn to introduce him to their Liberator from sin and death—Jesus Christ.

The Christian life is a battle, but in the end Jesus wins!

But thanks be to God, who gives us victory through our Lord Jesus Christ (1 Cor. 15:57).

But in all these things we overwhelmingly conquer through Him who loved us (Rom. 8:37).

Traveling Light

We live for a time as aliens in enemy territory (1 Peter 1:1; 2:11). Our spiritual citizenship is in heaven (Phil. 3:20). When final liberation comes in the ultimate sense, we can take nothing with us (Job 1:21; 1 Tim. 6:7). The only investment that lasts will be treasure stored up in heaven (Matt. 6:19-20). Our earthly roots need to be shallow and our anchor in this life should not be set too strongly.

In the ancient near east many of the inhabitants were sojourners or nomads. You can still see bedouins in the Middle East today, constantly moving, without a piece of property to call their own.

That too is our spiritual heritage for a time. Like Abraham (Heb. 11:8-10), David (Ps. 39:12-13), and even Jesus (Heb. 13:12-14), we must not become attached to this world because it will pass away. Our destiny is not here but in heaven.

Our family just received this letter from a fellow spiritual alien. Her experience speaks volumes about our sojourn behind enemy lines.

I lost my nursing license in 1988, had it suspended actually. I had cared for a multimillionaire bisexual, influential in the federal government, who developed AIDS. The summer of '87 was a long 4-month period and he was anxious to "talk about God." At the end, he thought he was dying and asked to see a pastor. I gave him my brother David's phone number and at his request, David came for 2½ hours.

The "lover" was furious and an ethical misconduct and breech of confidentiality complaint was lodged against me. It was taken to the Provincial Nursing Association who took me to a 6-day trial. They could find nothing wrong, except for this and decreed that my license be suspended until I had basic "refresher" training and submitted an essay stating why my Christian values and moral ethics clouded my nursing judgment when caring for an AIDS patient. Of course that is out of the question. I cannot deny the Lord that bought me, and so after thousands of dollars for legal fees, my earning capacity sank to $8,000 a year working part-time in a local department store selling carpets and lamps.

God never wastes our time or our tears. He could have changed the ruling but chose not to do so. Both patient and "lover" are now dead, but both knew the Way and the patient spent precious time with David who testified at the trial. When asked what he had discussed with the patient, he said that, "He asked of me the same questions that Nicodemus asked of the Lord that night. I explained that we are born into a family the first time by water, so the second time we are born into a family by the Spirit of God." The whole courtroom listened to him simply explain God's plan of salvation; and I am proud to have been there and lose my license for Jesus' sake. [6]

Looking Up

Jim Irwin, *Apollo 15* astronaut, came to a confirming and deepening faith in Christ because of his experience in space. Since those days, he has been used of God to take the Gospel around the world.

It's no wonder that he adopted the following poem as the symbol of his ministry. John Gillespie Magee, Jr., a British aviator who lost his life fighting in World War II, penned "High Flight." For Jim Irwin, for me, and for all who would pursue God, John Magee says it all, spiritually speaking.

Oh, I have slipped the surly bonds of earth
  And danced the skies on laughter-silvered wings;
Sunward I've climbed, and joined the tumbling mirth
  Of sun-split clouds — and done a hundred things

You have not dreamed of — wheeled and soared and swung
  High in the sunlit silence. Hov'ring there,
I've chased the shouting wind along, and flung
  My eager craft through footless halls of air.

Up, up the long, delirious, burning blue
  I've topped the windswept heights with easy grace
Where never lark, or even eagle flew.
  And, while with silent, lifting mind I've trod
The high untrespassed sanctity of space,
  Put out my hand and touched the face of God. [7]

STEP THREE

"GOING FOR BROKE"

*Not that I have already obtained it, or have already
become perfect, but I press on in order that I may lay hold
of that for which also I was laid hold of by Christ Jesus.
Brethren, I do not regard myself as having laid hold of
it yet; but one thing I do: forgetting what lies behind
and reaching forward to what lies ahead,
I press on toward the goal for the prize of the
upward call of God in Christ Jesus.
Philippians 3:12-14*

*C.T.'s life stands as some rugged Gibraltar—
a sign to all succeeding generations that it is
worthwhile to lose all this world can offer and
stake everything on the world to come. His life
will be an eternal rebuke to easy-going Christianity.
He has demonstrated what it means to follow Christ
without counting the cost and without looking back.[1]*
Alfred Buxton
C.T. Studd's co-pioneer
in Africa

I delight to do Thy will, O my God;
Thy Law is within my heart.
Psalm 40:8

9
KNOWING GOD'S WILL

Someone recently gifted me with a little porcelain message square. It reads, "Those who walk with God always reach their destination!" I've often thought since then that it could also be written, "Those who walk with God always reach *His* destination!" Isn't that the central truth of Jesus' invitation?

> *Come to Me, all who are weary and heavy-laden, and I will give you rest. Take My yoke upon you, and learn from Me, for I am gentle and humble in heart; and you shall find rest for your souls. For My yoke is easy, and My load is light (Matt. 11:28-30).*

Our bottom line in life ought to match God's bottom line. That's the way Jesus, the Son, lived in relationship to God, the Father. He told the disciples, "My food is to do the will of Him who sent Me, and to accomplish His work" (John 4:34). To the Jews, Jesus answered, "I do not seek My own will but the will of Him who sent Me" (5:30). The crowds in Galilee heard Him say, "For I have come down from heaven, not to do My own will, but the will of Him who sent Me" (6:38).

So, if we follow our Lord's example, God's will should frame and drive the priorities of our lives. If we obey His exhortation to join Him in His yoke, then we will walk in God's will. When we walk alongside the One who is consumed with doing the Heavenly Father's will, then His destination will be our destination.

Paul's passion for God's will moved him to pray that the believers in Colossae would be filled with the knowledge of His will in all spiritual wisdom and understanding (Col. 1:9). His prayer encompassed two elements of God's will: (1) that which is known by and is true of every Christian because Scripture reveals it; (2) God's personal will for us as individual Christians which will be discerned, understood, and affirmed through the process of life and passage of time.

Let's begin with the more obvious—God's will revealed in Scripture. Realize that while all of Scripture explains God's will, significant portions stand out because they explicitly state God's will. We want to examine ten such elements of God's will as basic training in godliness.

Salvation

All but four of the Bible's 1,189 chapters (Gen. 1–2 and Rev. 21–22) speak of God's salvation extended to all who would believe in Him through the Lord Jesus Christ. Only in Eden and eternity did or will the human race fully share in God's character of holiness without sin. So it is not surprising to read that it is God's desire or will for people to be saved from their sins (1 Tim. 2:4; 2 Peter 3:9).

Not only is it God's wish, but only by His will can people be saved (Gal. 1:3-5). He predestined us to salvation according to the kind intention of His will (Eph. 1:5) and then worked all things after the counsel of His will (1:11). James 1:18 says it best:

In the exercise of His will He brought us forth by the word of truth, so that we might be as it were the first fruits among His creatures.

One of the chief characteristics identifying one who truly knows God and is a part of His eternal family is a compulsion to know and do God's will. It highlights the salvation transaction. Jesus said, "For whoever does the will of God, he is My brother and sister and mother" (Mark 3:35). A spiritually inherited trait of one who has been born again into God's spiritual family is the lifestyle of doing God's will. So, the one who does God's will abides forever (Matt. 7:21; 1 John 2:17).

May I ask a personal question at this point? Have you ever admitted your spiritual bankruptcy, turned from your self- and sin-centered life, and asked God to forgive you through the Lord Jesus Christ, who died for your sins, rose from the grave on the third day, and extends the free gift of eternal life to all who would believe in Him? If you have, then proceed to the next step. If not, pause and prayerfully do so because you will be unable to take the next steps without having taken that first step out of Satan's dark domain into God's kingdom of light (Acts 26:18; Col. 1:13).

Sacrifice

Sociologist Bronislaw Malinowski notes, "Magic is when we manipulate the deities so that they perform our wishes; religion is when we subject ourselves to the will of the deities."[1] In a Christian context, the deceived address God as Lord but then pursue their own will, seemingly at God's expense. But not so the genuine Christian.

I urge you therefore, brethren, by the mercies of God, to present your bodies a living and holy sacrifice, acceptable to God, which is your spiritual service of worship. And do not be conformed to this world, but be transformed by the renewing of your mind, that you may prove what the will of

*God is, that which is good and acceptable and perfect
(Rom. 12:1-2).*

We have been saved by God's will to do God's will. In
some senses we are the human answer to Christ's prayer,
"Thy will be done, on earth as it is in heaven" (Matt. 6:10).

So it is reasonable then that we should present ourselves
as a "living sacrifice," since death has already taken place on
the cross when Christ died on our behalf (2 Cor. 5:15). Likewise, we should present ourselves as a "holy sacrifice" because Christ bore our sins in His body that we might live a
holy life (2 Cor. 6:14–7:1; Gal. 1:4; 1 Cor. 15:3; 1 Peter 2:24).

We mustn't jump off the altar, for only there can we experience and demonstrate that the will of God is good and acceptable and perfect. God will change us from the inside out
(transform us) rather than the world shaping us from without
(conform us).

Spirit Control

Read Paul's words, written to the Christians at Ephesus, very
carefully:

*So then do not be foolish, but understand what the will of
the Lord is. And do not get drunk with wine, for that is
dissipation, but be filled with the Spirit, speaking to one
another in psalms and hymns and spiritual songs, singing
and making melody with your heart to the Lord; always
giving thanks for all things in the name of our Lord Jesus
Christ to God, even the Father; and be subject to one another in the fear of Christ (Eph. 5:17-21).*

God's will involves God's Spirit literally controlling our
lives and giving us spiritual direction. How does He do this
and how can we cooperate in this spiritual venture? Look at
Colossians 3:16-17, and you'll discover that letting the Word
of God dwell in you richly produces the same spiritual quali-

ties as letting God's Spirit control you. The simple but profound conclusion is that God's Word energizes man's mind to obey God's Spirit.

If we do this, what will it produce? *First,* godly conversation (Eph. 5:19). We will communicate heavenward with songs of praise to God and horizontally to each other with words of spiritual joy. *Second,* a thankful reaction to all of life (5:20). *Third,* a submitted relationship to one another in the fellowship of Christ that will extend from our marriage and family life (5:22–6:4) into the work world (6:5-9) and beyond (6:10-20).

This answers the "how" and "what" raised by Peter's exhortation "to live the rest of the time in the flesh no longer for the lusts of men, but for the will of God" (1 Peter 4:2). We fuel the process by taking megadoses of God's Word. We check our progress by looking at three areas of life: (1) our rhetoric, (2) our reactions, and (3) our relationships. If you need a mentor in these areas, let Barnabas be your model (Acts 11:22-24).

Sanctification

Years ago my wife discipled a girl who attended a Christian college. Tragically, this young woman became pregnant outside of marriage and sought my counsel. I told her the first step to recovery involved confessing her immorality as sin against God (Gen. 39:9; Ps. 51:4).

Her response startled me. She blurted out that nowhere in Scripture did God expressly forbid intimate relationships between two people who were in love and intended to marry. I took her to a passage she apparently had overlooked or forgotten.

For this is the will of God, your sanctification; that is, that you abstain from sexual immorality; that each one of you know how to possess his own vessel in sanctification and honor (1 Thes. 4:3-4).

Nothing violates the holy character of God any more than impure conduct in the physical realm of life. It's true God created us sexual creatures (Gen. 1:27-28). He also gave us explicit directions in its exercise (Ex. 20:14, 17; Lev. 18; Matt. 5:27-28; 1 Cor. 7:1-5; Heb. 13:4). Any attitude or activity outside of these boundaries violates God's will. Sexual purity proves to be a basic measure of spiritual intimacy.

Submission
Apart from rebellion against God, the next two objects of disobedience tend to be governments and employers. Humanity chafes at their kind of authority. For Christians, God wills a different kind of response.

> *Submit yourselves for the Lord's sake to every human institution, whether to a king as the one in authority, or to governors as sent by him for the punishment of evildoers and the praise of those who do right. For such is the will of God that by doing right you may silence the ignorance of foolish men (1 Peter 2:13-15).*

> *Slaves, be obedient to those who are your masters according to the flesh, with fear and trembling, in the sincerity of your heart, as to Christ; not by way of eyeservice, as menpleasers, but as slaves of Christ, doing the will of God from the heart (Eph. 6:5-6).*

Whether we live in a somewhat free society like America or under a totalitarian system that characterized the Roman world of first-century Christianity, God wills obedience, with the obvious exception of obedience to man that is disobedience to God (Acts 5:27-29).

What can obedience to authority accomplish? It silences the ignorance of foolish men who otherwise would rail against God (1 Peter 2:15). It demonstrates the inner reality of your Christianity in an unmistakable way (Eph. 6:5-6). It provides eternal reward for what you have done (6:7-8).

A citizen's/employee's code of conduct should read:

GOD'S WILL
Nothing more,
Nothing less,
Nothing else.

Satisfaction

John Newton, former slave trader turned pastor, who wrote the beloved hymn "Amazing Grace," proclaimed as he died, "I am satisfied with the Lord's will."[2] In so saying, he not only issued a commentary on the Christian life but walked in God's will, even in his last moments on earth. As Paul writes, "In everything give thanks; for this is God's will for you in Christ Jesus." (1 Thes. 5:18).

Thanksgiving should surround a Christian walking in God's will. It should be:

1. In word .... Eph. 5:4; Col. 3:17
2. In deed .... Col. 3:17
3. In attitude ...... Col. 3:15
4. In prayer .... Phil. 4:6; Col. 4:2
5. In all things .... Eph. 5:20; 1 Thes. 5:18
6. At all times .... Eph. 5:20

A spirit of thanksgiving is not limited to America's annual November holiday called Thanksgiving. It's a 365-day-a-year experience. The great saints of old modeled a spirit of thanksgiving in some difficult circumstances.

Job blessed God's name even though he had just suffered the violent death of his children and servants plus the loss of his possessions (Job 1:21). After receiving an unjust but certain judgment of death, Daniel continued in his lifelong habit of thanking God three times daily (Dan. 6:10). Jesus knew His hour of crucifixion had come, but He took time with the disciples to give thanks to God (Matt. 26:27).

The apostles rejoiced that they had been considered worthy to suffer shame for Christ's name (Acts 5:41). Paul and Silas had been unjustly and illegally arrested and then incarcerated at Philippi, but they sang hymns of praise to celebrate (16:25).

What did all these people in diverse situations have in common? I believe they possessed an overwhelming sense of God's sovereign control of life and His goodness. No matter what happened, they could be genuinely thankful, satisfied that God's will was best.

Seeking

Our prayer life should be shaped by God's will. If the Spirit intercepts our prayers to edit them in conformity to God's will, then how much more should we labor to pray in God's will (Rom. 8:27). Our confidence in prayer can be measured by the certainty of praying in God's will.

And this is the confidence which we have before Him, that, if we ask anything according to His will, He hears us. And if we know that He hears us in whatever we ask, we know that we have the requests which we have asked from Him (1 John 5:14-15).

Paul prayed for the Colossians to know God's will (Col. 1:9). Epaphras prayed that they might stand perfect and fully assured in all the will of God (4:12).

Undoubtedly the most notable prayer with an emphasis on God's will came from the lips of God in human flesh. Jesus prayed in Gethsemane, "Father, if Thou art willing, remove this cup from Me; yet not My will, but Thine be done" (Luke 22:42). He prayed this model prayer asking that His will always be conformed to that of the Heavenly Father.

Where should you begin? Let me suggest that you start with the ten elements of God's will noted in this chapter. Pray that God's obvious will outlined in Scripture would characterize your life in Christ.

Serving

Tucked away in the Psalms is an instructive portion of Scripture: "Bless the Lord, all you His hosts, you who serve Him, doing His will" (Ps. 103:21).

The hosts of God, the ministering band of heavenly angels, serve according to the will of God.

So it was with Paul. In the introductions to five of his letters, he describes himself as "Paul, an apostle of Jesus Christ by the will of God" (1 Cor. 1:1; 2 Cor. 1:1; Eph. 1:1; Col. 1:1; 2 Tim. 1:1). In writing to the Romans, he noted on several occasions that he deeply desired to come and minister to them, but the will of God would ultimately determine his itinerary (Rom. 1:10; 15:32).

Our service should always be as an ambassador of Christ bidding to do His will on His behalf. That can cause frustration at times, particularly when we would like to be in a different location at another time in an alternative way than currently prescribed by God. That is a little like Mark Twain's commentary on God's Word and will. "It is not the parts of the Bible I don't understand that bother me, it's the parts I do understand." This old adage says it all, "Serve well where God plants you and let Him be concerned with your next transplant."

Suffering

Surprised? Let me relieve you by commenting that this is not for every Christian, but we should *all* be prepared. Peter, the apostle of suffering, teaches the truth he lived out.

For it is better, if God should will it so, that you suffer for doing what is right rather than for doing what is wrong (1 Peter 3:17).

Therefore, let those also who suffer according to the will of God entrust their souls to a faithful Creator in doing what is right (1 Peter 4:19).

121

There is no virtue in suffering for suffering's sake or for unrighteous behavior. But the highest commendation comes to one who suffers for Christ's cause. Jesus said, "Blessed are those who have been persecuted for the sake of righteousness" (Matt. 5:10). Antipas, a saint at Pergamum killed for Christ's sake, was addressed by Jesus as, "My witness, My faithful one" (Rev. 2:13).

It's a great honor to die serving one's country; patriotism of the highest order costs — even one's life. Our citizenship is in heaven and to die is gain (Phil. 1:21). How much more then should we be willing to suffer like our Saviour and enter more quickly into His heavenly glory (Heb. 10:32-39).

Shepherding

I am personally reminded again that the church is not mine but Christ's, and so is the ministry. Therefore, the church must adhere to His will, not mine. Peter wrote, "Shepherd the flock of God among you, exercising oversight not under compulsion, but voluntarily, according to the will of God" (1 Peter 5:2).

Kim Yardum Knight, my faithful secretary for over nine years, paused during a busy ministry day and asked me, "How would you define success?" After reflecting a moment and seeking God's wisdom, I replied, "Knowing God's will and walking in it."

That's the *sine qua non* of spiritual fruitfulness. Whether it be in the Christian life or in "full-time" ministry, we serve according to God's good will and for His pleasure (Phil. 2:12-13).

An Afterthought

These last few pages have really put us on notice. No longer can ignorance be our excuse for walking outside of God's will. We must submit our will to God's. Now, if you feel impatient to get on with "Finding God's Will," pause here a moment more.

Think about several implications of our study:

1. If one or more of these ten explicit statements of God's will is not your pattern of life, then you are out of God's will and God requires change.
2. Certainly we need to be more concerned with what we know than that which we seek to know. While God's personal will unfolds daily, concern yourself primarily with obeying what you know and letting the rest flow out of your maturing obedience.
3. Don't repeat the failure of Israel's disobedience to God's stated will. Count the cost!

Thus says the Lord, your Redeemer, the Holy One of Israel; "I am the Lord your God, who teaches you to profit, who leads you in the way you should go. If only you had paid attention to My commandments! Then your well-being would have been like a river, and your righteousness like the waves of the sea" (Isa. 48:17-18).

This prayer fittingly caps off our discussion of knowing God's will:

Now the God of peace, who brought up from the dead the great Shepherd of the sheep through the blood of the eternal covenant, even Jesus our Lord, equip you in every good thing to do His will, working in us that which is pleasing in His sight, through Jesus Christ, to whom be the glory forever and ever. Amen (Heb. 13:20-21).

Teach me to do Thy will,
for Thou art my God;
let Thy good Spirit lead
me on level ground.
Psalm 143:10

10
FINDING GOD'S WILL

For many, finding God's personal will at times seems like searching for something that is capriciously hidden, rarely knowable, or hopelessly lost. But not so for martyred missionary Jim Elliot. Read carefully this 1950 diary entry that expressed his sentiments toward determining God's specific will:

Impressed with Ephesians 5, "understanding what the will of the Lord is," and Romans 12, "proving what is the will of God." Every moment I may be conscious and rejoice in the knowledge of God's will. Obedience to every command puts me on the track and keeps me there. Decisions of course must be made, but as in railroad, so in life—a block signal, a crisis, is lighted only where there is special need. I may not always be in sight of a "go" light, but sticking to the tracks will take me where the next one is. Understanding the will of the Lord is believing Him, that

He will—in all situations where I have obeyed—make that way His own way, effectual for eternity.[1]

Problem

It's almost comical to hear the bizarre techniques to which Christians often resort to "squeeze" God's will out of Him. Perhaps the most frequent is the fleece method of Gideon (Jud. 6:36-40). Most do not realize that the fleece represented Gideon's lack of faith and insecurity, not to mention that God never commends "a fleece" to determine His will. Carefully consider this humble confession:

When we were teaching in Winnipeg, the Lord made it very clear that He wanted us to leave teaching to be involved in a local church ministry. At the same time, He made it abundantly clear that we were meant to come to Bethany Chapel in Calgary. It was undeniable guidance both for us and for the elders of the assembly in Calgary. Humanly speaking, the call was unexpected, but it came from God. But we had a house to sell in Winnipeg; so we put out a fleece. It was February, and we began to pray, "Lord, if You want us to go to Calgary, sell our house by April at such and such price." You know what? He did not! But we felt sure about His guidance, so we changed the fleece. "By June, Lord." Well, to make the story short, the house did not sell. In fact, it did not sell until the very Sunday in August when I first preached in Bethany Chapel, and at a price which meant we lost the equity we had in the house. What happened? Wasn't it God's will for us to come to Calgary? Yes, it was. We have never had clearer guidance in our lives about anything, and over and over God has confirmed that to us.

How did we know it was His will? After all, the fleece did not work. I believe God was teaching us not to trust in fleeces. But we knew His will, and that knowledge came by applying some basic principles.[2]

By trusting in the promises of God and applying some basic biblical principles, you too can confidently seek God's guidance. Whether it be in regard to your education, a job, whom you are to marry, where to live, or a myriad of other important life decisions, you can rest in the truth that God's will is always better than your own.

Promises

God is more concerned that we walk in His will than even we are. His Word contains numerous notes of encouragement to reassure us when we travel through life in heavy fog rather than on a clear, sunny day with perfect visibility.

Take courage with these six promises:

1. *Instruction*. . . . . I will instruct you and teach you in the way which you should go; I will counsel you with My eye upon you (Ps. 32:8).

2. *Counsel*. . . . . With Thy counsel Thou wilt guide me, and afterward receive me to glory (Ps. 73:24).

3. *Guidance*. . . . . For Thou art my rock and my fortress; for Thy name's sake Thou wilt lead me and guide me (Ps. 31:3).

4. *Direction*. . . . . Trust in the Lord with all your heart, and lean not on your own understanding; in all your ways acknowledge Him, and He shall direct your paths (Prov. 3:5-6, NKJV).

5. *Establishment*. . . . . . . Commit your works to the Lord, and your plans will be established (Prov. 16:3).

6. *Execution*. . . . . Commit your way to the Lord, trust also in Him, and He will do it (Ps. 37:5).

With God's precious and magnificent promises as our foundation, let's move on to what I have kiddingly called over the years "my 10 Ps in a pod" for affirming God's will. I have personally used them with great profit, particularly in determining God's ministry will in my life. No one principle alone gives clear direction, but the combined sense of direction usually proves unmistakable.

Principles

1. *Presentation.* "Present your bodies as a living and holy sacrifice . . . that you may prove what the will of God is, that which is good and acceptable and perfect" (Rom. 12:1-2).

Realizing that in Christ you are not your own—for you have been bought with a price (1 Cor. 6:19-20)—embrace the "anywhere, anytime, anything, at any cost" mindset. Be like Samuel (1 Sam. 3:10), Isaiah (Isa. 6:8), and Paul (Acts 22:10) who all were available to carry out God's will.

Unfortunately, some believe that presentation is like buying merchandise on approval. If I like it, I keep it; if not, I'll send it back. The Jews diligently sought God's will through Jeremiah (Jer. 42:2-3). But when Jeremiah revealed that God's will was not what the people had in mind, they called the prophet a liar and went their own way (43:1-4).

Don't be like Jonah, the wrong-way prophet, who headed in the opposite direction of God's will (Jonah 1:1-3). Rather, be like David, a man after God's own heart, who willed to do all of God's will (Acts 13:22).

2. *Prayer.* "And this is the confidence which we have before Him, that, if we ask anything according to His will, He hears us" (1 John 5:14).

Prayer should not be the last court of appeal but rather the first. As a child would seek parental guidance, so we should seek direction from our Heavenly Father.

Jesus expands on this wonderful truth in Luke 11:11-13:

Now suppose one of you fathers is asked by his son for a

fish; he will not give him a snake instead of a fish, will he? Or if he is asked for an egg, he will not give him a scorpion, will he? If you then, being evil, know how to give good gifts to your children, how much more shall your Heavenly Father give the Holy Spirit to those who ask Him?

We need not be shy, fearful, or insecure in praying. Rather we can be confident, even bold, to approach God and express our desire to know and walk in His will for our lives.

The late Paul Little recounted this incident from his life:

At the Urbana Convention in 1948, Dr. Norton Sterrett asked, "How many of you who are concerned about the will of God spend five minutes a day asking Him to show you His will?" It was as if somebody had grabbed me by the throat. At that time I was an undergraduate, concerned about what I should do when I graduated from the university. I was running around campus—going to this meeting, reading that book, trying to find somebody's little formula—1, 2, 3, 4 and a bell rings—and I was frustrated out of my mind trying to figure out the will of God. I was doing everything but getting into the presence of God and asking Him to show me. [3]

What about you?

3. *Principles.* "Thy word is a lamp to my feet, and a light to my path" (Ps. 119:105).

Martin Luther once noted that his conscience was tied to the Word of God. So should ours. Scripture contains the basics of God's will for us all. It contains the Beatitude attitudes (Matt. 5), the fruit of the Spirit (Gal. 5), the demonstration of love (1 Cor. 13), and the ultimate marks of spiritual maturity (1 Tim. 3). As we focus on making these character qualities the core of our lives, the rest will come in the right way and at the proper time.

We encounter trouble when we disregard the basics in

pursuit of the more advanced. Achan (Josh. 7:1-26), Ananias and Sapphira (Acts 5:1-11), and David (Ps. 32) could all tell about their brutal, short-circuiting experiences with God's revealed will. They now know that God's personal will does not bypass or nullify God's revealed will in Scripture.

President Hibben of Princeton once invited Buchman of the Oxford Movement to dinner.

Buchman, an eccentric believer in divine guidance, arrived late and unexpectedly brought three other men with him who had not been invited. When he shook hands with Mrs. Hibben, Buchman said, "The Lord told me to bring these three other men to dinner, too."

Mrs. Hibben, who had not expected the three added guests, replied, "Oh, I don't think the Lord had anything to do with it."

"Why not?" retorted Buchman.

"Because," Mrs. Hibben replied, "God is a gentleman."[4]

Make sure that what you claim to be God's will is in fact His will, not yours. The principles of Scripture can always test your claim.

4. *People.* "Without consultation, plans are frustrated, but with many counselors they succeed" (Prov. 15:22; see also 11:14; 20:18; 24:6).

Proverbs continually repeats the basic theme that input from other people to our lives proves invaluable. So does the "body" principle of the New Testament. "For the body is not one member, but many" (1 Cor. 12:14).

Paul needed Barnabas (Acts 9:26-27; 11:25), Peter needed Paul (Gal. 2:11-14), and the Israelite kings of the Old Testament needed their prophets and counselors. Unfortunately Rehoboam rejected the counsel of his court and split the kingdom (1 Kings 12:1-15).

Who are your counselors? Your pastor, perhaps, or elders in your church? Your spouse, a close Christian friend, or even your parents? A teacher, a Christian neighbor, or believer at work? Whomever they are, make sure they participate in your process of affirming God's will.

5. *Providence.* "And we know that God causes all things to work together for good to those who love God, to those who are called according to His purpose" (Rom. 8:28).

There's no better illustration of this than Paul's second missionary journey. He first thought his traveling partner would be Barnabas (who accompanied Paul on the first trip), but it turned out to be Silas and Timothy (Acts 15:39–16:3). Next, they wanted to continue west to Asia but the Holy Spirit forbade it (16:6). So they turned north to Bithynia but the Holy Spirit again rerouted them (16:7). Finally God called them to Macedonia (16:9-10).

That event in Paul's life should encourage us to know that, even for the great apostle, God's will had to be discerned by a process. Paul had two factors in his favor. One, he was available; two, he was in motion and thus easy to redirect.

Can you remember why Paul ministered on the island of Malta? Read about it in Acts 27:1–28:10. Paul never planned to be there but God providentially, through a great storm, directed his path there. You need to let God's Spirit, in harmony with unchangeable and unavoidable life experiences, be a major director in your odyssey called following God's will.

Here's a last word. Don't be dismayed if it makes more sense looking back than ahead. A Puritan pastor once observed, "The providence of God is like Hebrew words — it can be read only backwards."[5]

6. *Patience.* "But do not let this one fact escape your notice, beloved, that with the Lord one day is as a thousand years, and a thousand years as one day" (2 Peter 3:8; see also Ps. 90:4).

God's concept of time differs radically from our human perception. He created the world in seven days and the world has ever since insisted it took millions if not billions of years. On the other hand, He has been lovingly patient with the human race in allowing thousands of years of history to believe in Him when He could have brought swift judgment much earlier.

Typically, God's time frame moves slower than ours. On more than one occasion the psalmist cried out, "How long, O Lord?" (Ps. 13:1-2; see also Ps. 6:3; 35:17; 62:3; 74:10; 79:5; 80:4; 82:2; 89:46; 90:13; 94:3) If Moses had waited (Acts 7:24-25), or Saul (1 Sam. 13:8-14), or Israel (Num. 21:4-6), biblical history would have been written differently.

Jesus certainly was patient with God's clock. He knew when His time had not yet come (John 7:6) and did not act prematurely. On the other hand, when the hour arrived, He moved (Matt. 26:18). He always had a keen sense of the difference between the immediate and ultimate will of God.

If God is not moving fast enough for you, then slow down and don't run ahead. Allow God's Spirit to manifest His fruit of patience in your life (Gal. 5:22-23). Then agree with the early church, "If the Lord wills, we shall live and also do this or that" (James 4:15).

7. *Persistence.* "Now He was telling them a parable to show that at all times they ought to pray and not to lose heart" (Luke 18:1).

This story of the nasty judge and needy widow drives home the point of perseverance, particularly in prayer. Don't quit; keep on seeking God's direction.

Beware that there is a wrong kind of "pressing on." Balaam continued to follow the path of disobedience even when God told him to stop (Num. 22:21-35). But if no barriers block the way, then continue your quest. Even if you have a false start or two, you can be ultimately rewarded like John Mark (compare Acts 13:13 and 15:37-38 with 2 Tim. 4:11). Continue until God makes it clear that you are to stop, like Paul who prayed three times for the thorn to be removed before he accepted it as God's will (2 Cor. 12:7-10).

By this time you might be asking, "How do I draw any conclusions from these principles?" Start looking for common points of agreement or intersection. When they come together and agreement exists among most, then you will begin to see the pattern emerge. If your circumstances are taking a lengthy time, I would recommend you keep a diary so that you can easily remember, review, and reflect on each element and its relationship to the others.

8. *Proceed.* "He who is holy, who is true, who has the key of David, who opens and no one will shut, and who shuts and no one opens" (Rev. 3:7).

There's a time to slack off and a time to surge ahead. So be discerning. Don't move forward to go through a door which God has closed, because you will never open it. Israel tried and failed miserably (Num. 14:26-45).

On the other hand, the church at Philadelphia had only a little power, but they proceeded through the God-opened door that no one could shut (Rev. 3:8). The Asian and Bithynian doors were closed to Paul (Acts 16:6-7), so he marched through the Macedonian door (16:10ff).

In counseling, I always ask two questions before making any commitments. First, "Are you seeking God's will?" Second, "When we find it, will you proceed with it?" Only if both questions receive a strong "Yes!" will I continue. It becomes extraordinarily frustrating to put the brakes on someone who plunges ahead in wild disregard for God's will; it's equally painful to try and blast someone into motion when the time and direction of God's will are obvious.

9. *Peace.* "Be anxious for nothing, but in everything by prayer and supplication with thanksgiving let your requests be made known to God. And the peace of God which surpasses all comprehension, shall guard your hearts and your minds in Christ Jesus" (Phil. 4:6-7).

Paul and Silas, while in the Philippian jail, experienced that peace (Acts 16:25). So did Peter in the Jerusalem prison (12:6). But it's not always as we might imagine it as if Hollywood filmed the situation.

I received this note of encouragement from the president of a major, conservative seminary in America. It really strikes the balance and rings with reality:

I am confident that your decision to remain at Grace Community Church was prayerfully made, and that you are sensitive to the Lord's leading in your life. Knowing the will of God is not as easy to understand as some of the "manuals" would have us believe, is it? My own experience has been that the clear-cut, "open and shut" cases are few and far between. It is far more difficult to choose between several opportunities, each of which has great potential. Sometimes all we can do after prayer and reflection is choose one and then see if God gives us reassuring peace. I have also found that that "peace" doesn't always come at once. In fact, my study of Bible personalities indicates that even those who apparently were in the center of God's will did not experience uninterrupted joy and peace in their circumstances. I guess it all boils down to the fact that in this world we are in a battle, and battles are not noted for being easy. [6]

10. *Praise.* "In everything give thanks; for this is God's will for you in Christ Jesus" (1 Thes. 5:18).

Regardless of how hopeless the task seems, how foggy the circumstances become, or how long it takes, continue to thank God for who He is and what He is doing in your life. Then live one day at a time fully trusting God with your future.

Postscript

Never forget that God's will is good and acceptable and perfect. If the situation looks bleak, the problem rests with us, not God. We must walk by faith and not always by sight (2 Cor. 5:7).

R.C. Chapman offers this overarching principle:

The rule that governs my life is this: Anything that dims my vision of Christ, or takes away my taste for Bible study, or cramps my prayer life, or makes Christian work difficult is wrong for me, and I must as a Christian turn away from it. [7]

So, by unreserved presentation coupled with uncompromising obedience and unconditional trust, pursue God's will with a holy passion.

In so doing, remember:

God's will will never take you where God's grace cannot keep you.

Great is the Lord, and highly to be praised;
and His greatness is unsearchable.
One generation shall praise Thy works to another,
and shall declare Thy mighty acts.
Psalm 145:3-4

11
GRASPING GOD'S GREATNESS

Former heavyweight boxing champion Muhammad Ali claimed, "I'm the greatest!" Sports fans continually chant, "We're number one!" But regardless of what other people think or say, God alone is great.

This hypothetical scene set by Dr. S.M. Lockridge vividly portrays God's greatness:

Where did God come from? He came from nowhere! The reason God came from nowhere is that there was nowhere for Him to come from. Coming from nowhere, He stood on nothing. The reason He had to stand on nothing is there was nowhere for Him to stand. And standing on nothing, He reached out where there was nowhere to reach and caught something where there was nothing to catch and hung something on nothing and He told it to stay there. Now standing on nothing, He took the hammer of His own will; He struck the anvil of His omnipotence and sparks

*flew. He caught them on the tips of His fingers, flung them
out into space and bedecked the heaven with stars, but no
one said a word. The reason no one said anything is that
there was nobody there to say anything. So God Himself
said, "That is very good."*[1]

The Majesty of God's Greatness

With God, there are no boundaries to His presence, no limits
to His knowledge, and no governor on His power. The person
of God defines "greatness."

We're reminded four times in Scripture of our response to
God's greatness. "Great is the Lord and greatly to be
praised" (1 Chron. 16:25; Ps. 48:1; 96:4; 145:3). Nehemiah
described God's greatness with terms like *awesome* and *mighty*
(Neh. 9:32), as did Daniel (Dan. 9:4) and Jeremiah (Jer.
32:18).

David's prayers habitually acknowledged God's greatness:

*For this reason Thou art great, O Lord God; for there is
none like Thee, and there is no God besides Thee, according to all that we have heard with our ears (2 Sam. 7:22).*

*Thine, O Lord, is the greatness and the power and the
glory and the victory and the majesty, indeed everything
that is in the heavens and the earth; Thine is the dominion, O Lord, and Thou dost exalt Thyself as head over all
(1 Chron. 29:11).*

Other Scripture describes: (1) God's great power (Eph.
1:19); (2) God's great promises (2 Peter 1:4); (3) God's great
kingdom (Dan. 7:27); and (4) God's great faithfulness (Lam.
3:23).

"Majesty" also links synonymously with "greatness," as
the following passages demonstrate:

The Lord reigns, He is clothed with majesty; the Lord has

clothed and girded Himself with strength; indeed, the world is firmly established, it will not be moved (Ps. 93:1).

For we did not follow cleverly devised tales when we made known to you the power and coming of our Lord Jesus Christ, but we were eyewitnesses of His majesty. For when He received honor and glory from God the Father, such an utterance as this was made to Him by the Majestic Glory, "This is My beloved Son with whom I am well pleased" (2 Peter 1:16-17).

And He is the radiance of His glory and the exact representation of His nature, and upholds all things by the word of His power. When He had made purification of sins, He sat down at the right hand of the Majesty on high (Heb. 1:3).

We'll better understand the dimensions of God's greatness by examining the macro-world of space and the micro-world of the human body. Psalm 8:1-4 points to the heavens and Psalm 139:13-16 speaks of our being fearfully and wonderfully made in the womb. These illustrations will help us to grasp, but never completely comprehend, the fullness of our great God.

To grasp the scene, imagine a perfectly smooth glass pavement on which the finest speck can be seen. Then shrink our sun from 865,000 miles in diameter to only two feet . . . and place the ball on the pavement to represent the sun. Step off 82 paces (about two feet per pace), and to represent proportionately the first planet, Mercury, put down a tiny mustard seed.

Take 60 steps more, and for Venus put an ordinary BB.

Mark 78 more steps . . . put down a green pea representing Earth.

Step off 108 paces from there, and for Mars put down a pinhead.

Sprinkle around some fine dust for the asteroids, then

take 788 steps more. For Jupiter, place an orange on the glass at that spot.

After 934 more steps, put down a golf ball for Saturn.

Now it gets really involved. Mark 2,086 steps more, and for Uranus... a marble.

Another 2,322 steps from there you arrive at Neptune. Let a cherry represent Neptune.

This will take two and a half miles, and we haven't even discussed Pluto! If we swing completely around, we have a smooth glass surface five miles in diameter, yet just a tiny fraction of the heavens—excluding Pluto. On this surface, five miles across, we have only a seed, BB, pea, pinhead, some dust, an orange, golf ball, a marble, and a cherry. Guess how far we'd have to go on the same scale before we could put down another two-foot ball to represent the nearest star. Come on, guess. Seven hundred paces? Two thousand steps more? Four thousand four hundred feet? No, you're way off.

We'd have to go 6,720 miles before we could arrive at that star. Miles, not feet. And that's just the first star among millions. In one galaxy among perhaps thousands, maybe billions. And all of it in perpetual motion... the most accurate timepiece known to man.[2]

Consider your body which proves microscopic compared to our solar system but no less intricate in detail. God made you with over 200 bones plus more than 630 muscles. Your body contains over 30 trillion cells, 16 billion nerve endings, and 4 million pain sensors. Our lungs contain 750 million air sacs and take about 24,000 breaths every 24 hours. Blood flows 168 million miles daily in our bodies, pumped by our heart which beats over 100,000 times a day.[3]

No wonder the heavens and the human body point unmistakably to God's creative power and greatness.

So great is God's greatness that He will not tolerate anyone who tries to elbow into His exclusive domain. The Philis-

tines tried and painfully backed away (1 Sam. 5:1-12). Nebuchadnezzar, the seventh-century B.C. Babylonian king who
ruled the world, tried but retreated in embarrassment (Dan.
4:1-37). Herod Agrippa II tried also and God took his life with
worms (Acts 12:21-23).

Job lived to be called "the greatest of all the men of the
east" (Job 1:3). But one day tragedy struck and robbed him of
his perceived greatness. He lost his children, servants, possessions, dignity, health, and prominence among men. God
then gave Job a lesson on "greatness." We would do well to
learn from Job's experience, so that we do not have to personally repeat it. He quickly learned that God, not man,
serves as the measure of greatness.

There were two sessions—the first in Job 38:1–40:5 and
the last in 40:6–42:6. They follow this pattern:

God's challenge........38:3 and 40:6-7
God's test ....38:4–40:2 and 40:8–41:34
Job's conclusion ....40:3-5 and 42:1-6

Take time to read the scenes as if you were Job being
questioned by God. See if you don't begin to both understand
and experience something of the One who is uniquely and
majestically great.

The Marks of Human Greatness
Man's definition of greatness involves largeness in size or
number, remarkableness in magnitude or effect, and superi-
ority in character or quality. It's often measured by appear-
ance, dollars, power, ability, genealogy, position, accomplish-
ment, or possessions. The terms Who's Who, All-American,
World Champion, Olympian, World-Class, All-Pro, or Guinness
record-holder might apply.

The human race makes a "great" mistake to think this
way. Jesus' disciples proved no exception. They frequently
focused on who among themselves was greatest (Matt. 18:1;
20:20-28; Mark 9:33-34; 10:37; Luke 9:46; 22:24; John 13:16).
So did the Corinthians in reference to Paul, Apollos, and

Cephas. (1 Cor. 1:10-17). Both Jesus and Paul put the discussion in perspective.

He said to them, "My cup you shall drink; but to sit on My right and on My left, this is not Mine to give, but it is for those for whom it has been prepared by My Father" (Matt. 20:23).

But we have this treasure in earthen vessels, that the surpassing greatness of the power may be of God and not from ourselves (2 Cor. 4:7).

While there will never be an earthly counterpart to the eternal greatness of God, the Bible does speak about four marks of kingdom greatness that bear "great" similarity to God's character. These then are the marks of human greatness as defined by God who alone is great.

Mark #1—Scripturalness. "Whoever then annuls one of the least of these commandments, and so teaches others, shall be called least in the kingdom of heaven; but whoever keeps and teaches them, he shall be called great in the kingdom of heaven" (Matt. 5:19).

God's Word cannot be broken (John 10:35) because it is a total package. To disallow, annul, or disobey one part is to be guilty of all (James 2:10).

The Jews used to pride themselves in keeping the Law down to the smallest detail. Some rabbis believed the Deuteronomy 22:6-7 statute concerning a mother bird and her chick was the least in importance. Jesus commented on the Pharisees' habit of tithing mint, dill, and cumin (Lev. 27:30; Matt. 23:23).

What might seem commendable at first, Jesus condemned. Why? Because while fulfilling the minutia of the Law, they neglected the more important matters. They did not keep the whole counsel of God (Matt. 28:20; Acts 20:27). Those who teach and live this way are least in God's kingdom.

The greatest, however, shall first keep or obey and then teach others all of the commandments. The priority of living and *then* communicating is reinforced elsewhere in Scripture (Ezra 7:10; 1 Tim. 4:16). That's why James warns: "Let not many of you become teachers, my brethren, knowing that as such we shall incur a stricter judgment" (James 3:1).

God's view of you is directly proportional to your view of Him. It's evidenced by our commitment to live out and teach others His Word. To be great is to intellectually and obediently embrace all of Scripture.

Mark #2—Submissiveness. "At that time the disciples came to Jesus, saying, 'Who then is greatest in the kingdom of heaven?' And He called a child to Himself and set him before them, and said, 'Truly I say to you, unless you are converted and become like children, you shall not enter the kingdom of heaven. Whoever then humbles himself as this child, he is the greatest in the kingdom of heaven' " (Matt. 18:1-4).

Humility, or the absence of pride, marks a "great" convert to God's kingdom.

But He gives a greater grace. Therefore it says, "God is opposed to the proud, but gives grace to the humble" (James 4:6).

He has told you, O man, what is good; and what does the Lord require of you but to do justice, to love kindness, and to walk humbly with your God? (Micah 6:8)

Everyone who is proud in heart is an abomination to the Lord; assuredly, he will not be unpunished (Prov. 16:5).

Submission to God's Word and the imitation of Christ's incarnate, humble character identifies "great" kingdom citizens (Phil. 2:5-8).

Mark #3—Service. "But the greatest among you shall be your servant" (Matt. 23:11).

This is just the opposite of the way we think—authority not responsibility, strength not weakness, and power not character.

Jesus is the model Teacher/Servant (Matt. 20:28). He came to give, not get; to pay, not receive. We should follow Him. Greatness is not being carried off the field of victory by a cheering throng. Rather, the victor carries off those who would otherwise have lost had he not served them.

Mark #4—Sacrifice. "But now abide faith, hope, love, these three; but the greatest of these is love" (1 Cor. 13:13).

Faith and hope are unseen—love deals with the visible. Faith looks back to the past, hope to the future, but love is now. The love of which Paul writes is love rendered without being prompted and love that expects nothing in return. That is kingdom greatness. It involves the fifteen action qualities mentioned in 1 Corinthians 13:4-7. Living these out as a pattern of life makes a Christian great. On the other hand, their absence makes one nothing (13:1-3).

Let me share with you a touching eulogy delivered at a service over which I presided on a windy, fall day in the San Fernando Valley. It was delivered by the older brother of a blind, mentally impaired young man who died of cancer. Here's the essence of human greatness as measured by God:

What can be said of the life of Ronald Castersen? Well, it all depends on the way you look at it. From one point of view, he had no great abilities or contributions to society. He was not a well known person, and for sure will never be found in any history books.

But history books are not the only books being written. God is also keeping a book. And who has He chosen to be logged into this book? First Corinthians 1:27-29 says, "But God has chosen the foolish things of the world to shame the wise, and God has chosen the weak things of the world to shame the things which are strong, and the base things of the world and the despised, God has chosen the things that are not, that He might nullify the things that are, that no man should boast before God." Ronald's life was very valuable to God, indeed He even sent His own Son to die for him.

Ronald enjoyed the simple things of life. He always loved children, in fact I can remember him sitting in the front yard with his box full of candy generously giving it out to the children who came by. He knew that it was better to give than to receive, and this unselfish attitude was always a strong characteristic of his life.

He wasn't one to complain either. Legally blind from the age of 12, I never can remember him saying, "I wish I wasn't blind." In fact he was always one that would encourage others that were in a difficult situation that God was enough for whatever their need might be.

He loved also to work. His condition didn't allow him to do things that were very strenuous, but he was always up early to go to the workshop where he kept busy with various odd jobs. He loved to do small tasks around the house as much as he was capable of.

The greatest attribute that Ronald had in his life was his simple love and reverence for God. He came to know the Lord Jesus as his Saviour as a young boy and loved to tell others about Him also. That is what makes this a joyful time. True, it is a time of sorrow because we miss him, but a great joy because he has graduated from this life and has entered into the joy of the Lord. He has regained his sight. Someday his body will be resurrected from the dead, and we know we will see him again.

I know Ron was a real example to me. Also I thank God for the privilege of knowing him for 26 years. Before I was a Christian he wouldn't give me theological explanations, he would just tell me, "That's sin," when he knew something was sin. He knew his God and I'm sure his example was very instrumental in my having gotten saved, for which I thank God.

On Sunday mornings he was always up before me, enthusiastically waking me up, "Come on, Steve, let's go worship the Lord."

Yes, in ways he was poor in this world, but thank God he had "treasure in heaven, where moth and rust cannot corrupt, and thieves do not break in and steal."[4]

The Mandates of Kingdom Greatness

I once saw this sign in a "left-handed" shop in Southern California. "Everyone is born right-handed, only the great overcome it!" According to the entrepreneur who originated that bit of creative advertisement, only those who live "the southpaw way" are great.

God's perspective points in a different direction. Those with "great" character and conduct will focus on God's "great" cause. According to Jesus this can be summarized in two "great" activities.

1. *The Great Commandments.* "And one of the scribes came and heard them arguing and . . . asked Him, 'What commandment is the foremost of all?' Jesus answered, 'The foremost is, "Hear, O Israel; the Lord our God is one Lord; and you shall love the Lord your God with all your heart, and with all your soul, and with all your mind, and with all your strength." The second is this, "You shall love your neighbor as yourself." There is no other commandment greater than these' " (Mark 12:28-31).

The 613 individual commandments of the Mosaic Law reduce to 2—love God, love man (Deut. 6:5; Lev. 19:18). If we love God, we'll love to obey and teach all of His will contained in His Word. If we love men, we'll demonstrate our love for God to them by submission, service, and sacrifice.

Two young brothers once discussed their life goals. One wanted to be rich and famous while the other simply desired to obey Christ fully. Both reached their goal. But in the end, the first was remembered only by the second's achievements. The epitaph on the rich brother's tombstone read,

"Here lies the brother of David Livingstone."

"Great" people manifest God's great love in their lives both for God and for other human beings.

2. *The Great Commission.* The term *great commission* is never used in Scripture. However, it is a fitting title to describe Christ's final instructions to the disciples and in turn to all Christians until Jesus returns. Note the apostles' various renderings of this divine mandate:

> *But the eleven disciples proceeded to Galilee, to the mountain which Jesus had designated. And when they saw Him, they worshiped Him; but some were doubtful. And Jesus came up and spoke to them, saying, "All authority has been given to Me in heaven and on earth. Go therefore and make disciples of all the nations, baptizing them in the name of the Father and the Son and the Holy Spirit, teaching them to observe all that I commanded you; and lo, I am with you always, even to the end of the age" (Matt. 28:16-20).*

> *And He said to them, "Go into all the world and preach the Gospel to all creation" (Mark 16:15).*

> *And He said to them, "Thus it is written, that the Christ should suffer and rise again from the dead the third day; and that repentance for forgiveness of sins should be proclaimed in His name to all the nations, beginning from Jerusalem. You are witnesses of these things" (Luke 24:46-48).*

> *Jesus therefore said to them again, "Peace be with you; as the Father has sent Me, I also send you." And when He had said this, He breathed on them, and said to them, "Receive the Holy Spirit. If you forgive the sins of any, their sins have been forgiven them; if you retain the sins of any, they have been retained" (John 20:21-23).*

> *But you shall receive power when the Holy Spirit has come*

upon you; and you shall be My witnesses both in Jerusalem, and in all Judea and Samaria, and even to the remotest part of the earth (Acts 1:8).

The Lord Jesus Christ calls Christians to the greatest of causes—the kingdom of God. The priority activities are:

- *Going*
- *Making disciples*
- *Baptizing*
- *Teaching complete obedience*

Sometimes we take this call to be optional, or to be discussed but never embraced. Not so! The Great Commission must be understood in a military sense. Christ's orders do *not* form the basis for dialogue but rather obedience.

Listen to the testimony of John Wesley who took Christ's words as his personal obligation:

I look upon all the world as my parish; thus far I mean, that in whatever part of it I am I judge it meet, right, and my bounden duty to declare, unto all that are willing to hear, the glad tidings of salvation. [5]

Paul prayed for the Philippians:

And this I pray, that your love may abound still more and more in real knowledge and all discernment, so that you may approve the things that are excellent, in order to be sincere and blameless until the day of Christ (Phil. 1:9-10).

Discerning Christians will always choose the excellence of the Great Commandments and the Great Commission when God's will prevails in their lives.

Models of Godly Greatness

Interestingly, God does not look for great people to manifest His greatness. Neither Israel (Deut. 7:6-8) nor the church

(1 Cor. 1:26-31) were chosen because of existing greatness, but rather just the opposite—because of "great" need.

Some of God's great saints have been well known; others lived in obscurity. Paul saw himself as the greatest of sinners and the least of saints (1 Tim. 1:15; Eph. 3:8). Job (Job 1:1, 3), Ruth (Ruth 3:11), Apollos (Acts 18:27-28), and Daniel (Dan. 10:11, 19) are each called "great" in Scripture.

Two other names stand out among the many. First is David, a young shepherd boy who was nothing but to whom God promised "a great name, like the name of the great men who are on the earth" (2 Sam. 7:9). Second is John the Baptist of whom Jesus said, "Among those born of women there has not arisen anyone greater than John" (Matt. 11:11).

My favorite Bible "great" is Igdaliah. Chances are that you've never heard a message preached on him; maybe you've never heard of him at all! He represents the majority of committed Christians who live in relative obscurity by comparison to the famous few. Such was the case of Igdaliah whom God refers to in Jeremiah 35:4 as "the man of God." Appropriately, *Igdaliah* in Hebrew means "God is great." He bore the name that marked his life.

A Parting Word

I once read a sign that said, "If Moses had a committee, the Jews would still be in Egypt!" God doesn't use great committees but He does enlist great commitment.

Someone asked Francis of Assisi why he accomplished so much. He replied, "The Lord looked down from heaven upon the earth and said, 'Where can I find the weakest, the littlest, the meanest man on the face of the earth?' Then He saw me and said, 'Now I've found him, and I will work through him. He won't be proud of it. He'll see that I'm only using him because of his littleness and insignificance.' "

I'm not Assisi or David or John the Baptist. Maybe you aren't either. But we can pray to be Igdaliahs—weak vessels that contain the greatness of God.

Thou wilt make known to me the path of life;
in Thy presence is fulness of joy;
in Thy right hand there are pleasures forever.
Psalm 16:11

12
PLEASING GOD

Having just flown home to Los Angeles from Pittsburgh, I rushed to make a seminary graduation speaking engagement. My opening remarks focused on an unusual event from the just completed flight.

Our 737 lost power to an engine and the plane dipped in the direction of difficulty. During the ensuing confusion, I heard the man next to me pray, "Lord, if You get me back alive, I will give You half of all I own." The pilot in the meantime had quickly corrected the problem and we continued toward our destination without further incident. But I couldn't get the man's promise out of my mind.

Once in the terminal after landing, I came alongside him and joked, "Sir, I am a representative of God and I'm here to collect your promise to Him." Without missing a beat he replied, "Oh, I've made a new vow. I told God that if I'm foolish enough to fly again, I will give Him *all* that I own." So much for that opportunity!

Now tell me—who was this man trying to please? Himself or God? Admittedly, the story in fact is fiction but oh-so-true in spirit. It typifies the heart of self-centered, self-pleasing mankind whose driving bent focuses inward for self, not upward toward God. It's the spirit of our age; and it's out of sync with the Spirit of God. "Thou art worthy, O Lord, to receive glory and honor and power: for Thou hast created all things, and for Thy pleasure they are and were created" (Rev. 4:11, KJV).

The Apostle Paul warns that this problem will intensify as time progresses, for in the last days people will be lovers of pleasure rather than lovers of God (2 Tim. 3:1-4). James condemns self-pleasure as counterproductive to our prayer lives: "You ask and do not receive, because you ask with wrong motives, so that you may spend it on your pleasures" (James 4:3).

God finds no pleasure in mere religious ritual (Ps. 40:6; Heb. 10:6, 8). Nor is He pleased with those who insist on walking by sight rather than according to faith (Heb. 10:38). The degree of spiritual intimacy that we share with God depends uniquely on whom we make our object of pleasure.

God's Pleasure

"I feel sorry for you, Dick. You will not be able to please everyone." During the first week of a new ministry I heard those words from a well-meaning and perceptive member of the flock. My reply went something like this, "That may be true, but I only want to please God." I would rather know God's pleasure at the expense of man's satisfaction than the reverse.

Why? For two reasons. First, I do not want to compete with God for He will do (in spite of me or you) what He pleases. I desire to move with Him, not against Him.

But our God is in the heavens; He does whatever He pleases (Ps. 115:3).

My purpose will be established, and I will accomplish all My good pleasure (Isa. 46:10).

Second, I want to cooperate with God who, in Christ, gave me eternal life. Pleasing Him is an important part of my new faith relationship with God.

For it is God who is at work in you, both to will and to work for His good pleasure (Phil. 2:13).

Now the God of peace, who brought up from the dead the great Shepherd of the sheep through the blood of the eternal covenant, even Jesus our Lord, equip you in every good thing to do His will, working in us that which is pleasing in His sight, through Jesus Christ, to whom be the glory forever and ever. Amen (Heb. 13:20-21).

Too many Christians are like the elderly man who was traveling with a boy and a donkey. As they walked through a village, the man was leading the donkey and the boy was walking behind. The townspeople said the old man was a fool for not riding, so to please them he climbed up on the animal's back. When they came to the next village, the people said the old man was cruel to let the child walk while he enjoyed the ride. So, to please them, he got off and set the boy on the animal's back and continued on his way. In the third village, people accused the child of being lazy for making the old man walk, and the suggestion was made that they both ride. So the man climbed on and they set off again. In the fourth village, the townspeople were indignant at the cruelty to the donkey because he was made to carry two people. The frustrated man was last seen carrying the donkey down the road.

Unless our concentrated focus is upon pleasing God, we too will become spiritually frustrated. Pleasing others or pleasing self falls incredibly short of the spiritual epitome to please God and, in that desire, to also find our own chief source of pleasure. If we seek God and that which His hand provides, we will experience the blessed pleasures of our Lord (Ps. 16:11).

Our Passion

General Omar Bradley in a 1948 Armistice Day address noted, "We have too many men of science, too few men of God. We have grasped the mystery of the atom and rejected the Sermon on the Mount." Over four decades have passed and we still face the same spiritual vacuum—too many people pleasing themselves and too few people pleasing God.

It's similar to the time of Malachi. That Old Testament prophet wrote:

A son honors his father, and a servant his master. Then if I am a father, where is My honor? And if I am a master, where is My respect? says the Lord of hosts to you, O priests who despise My name. But you say, "How have we despised Thy name?" You are presenting defiled food upon My altar. But you say, "How have we defiled Thee?" In that you say, "The table of the Lord is to be despised." But when you present the blind for sacrifice, is it not evil? And when you present the lame and sick, is it not evil? Why not offer it to your governor? Would he be pleased with you? Or would he receive you kindly? says the Lord of hosts (Mal. 1:6-8).

The unmistakable symptom of the spiritually anemic or dead community is desiring more honor for humanity than for God (note the church at Sardis, Rev. 3:1-3).

The exhortation of Scripture gives us a totally different perspective. "For you were formerly darkness, but now you are light in the Lord; walk as children of light . . . trying to learn what is pleasing to the Lord" (Eph. 5:8, 10). The *King James Version* translates the Greek word for *pleasing* as *ac-*

ceptable. Don't miss the point—that which is acceptable to God is also pleasing. There is no middle ground, for if it is unacceptable, it is also displeasing. Only obedience to the truth of God is acceptable, and this alone pleases, delights, and brings joy.

When I served in Vietnam as the pilot of an air cushion vehicle and later as an operational briefer for Vice Admiral Elmo Zumwalt, I had one passion—to please my commanding officer. Daily I experienced an internal ignition that produced external energy which focused on doing those acceptable things that brought pleasure to my leader. By the way, when the Master is pleased, your own life will also become more pleasurable.

Paul writes with a military environment in mind. "No soldier in active service entangles himself in the affairs of everyday life, so that he may please the one who enlisted him as a soldier" (2 Tim. 2:4).

It's a matter of priorities. You and I must decide who and what is most important—God and His kingdom or me and my world. There are no alternatives for Christians. Since God enlisted us into His "kingdom corps," we are soldiers of the Lord and must focus on pleasing Him. Like the centurion, we must be under authority (Matt. 8:8-9) because it is impossible to serve both God and mammon (6:24-34). We must choose today whom we will serve (Josh. 24:15).

That's why Paul writes with transparent honesty about the aim of his life. "Therefore also we have as our ambition, whether at home or absent, to be pleasing to Him" (2 Cor. 5:9). Bury forever the lie that Christians can't be ambitious. The issue is not ambition, rather the object and purpose of our ambition.

The Greek word for *ambition,* translated *labor* in the *King James Version* and *goal* in the *New International Version,* carries the literal idea of seeking that which is honorable with an attitude of love. Seeking the priorities of God ranks as the highest and most honorable of ambitions. Thus, we can anticipate a time of reward at the Judgment Seat of Christ (2 Cor. 5:10). Check out your passion level. Maybe it needs to be stoked up a couple of notches.

If you want to know what it will sound like when applied to life, listen to one of the deputy fire chiefs in Los Angeles who wrote me these unforgettable lines: "Being a fireman is sufficient to fill the limit of my ambitions in life and to make me serve the general purpose of human society—BUT!! only to the degree that I can sense the Lord's presence, guidance, and approval of that ambition."[1]

The Biblical Pattern

How can we who have little bring pleasure to God who has everything? Answer: As an obedient child brings pleasure to a parent. No matter how inadequate or insufficient, God takes great pleasure in our obedience and growth.

It all begins with faith—the overarching principle in pleasing God. "And without faith it is impossible to please Him, for he who comes to God must believe that He is, and that He is a rewarder of those who seek Him" (Heb. 11:6). Faith is indispensable both to salvation and to spiritual intimacy (Col. 2:6).

Here are some childlike steps of faith you can take which will please God because they evidence spiritual health:

1. *Spiritual commitment.* After spending eleven chapters developing doctrinal truths about salvation, Paul exhorts the Romans to decisive action: "I urge you therefore, brethren, by the mercies of God, to present your bodies a living and holy sacrifice, acceptable to God, which is your spiritual service of worship" (Rom. 12:1).

The first act is sacrifice—not dead but living. It will be acceptable and pleasing to God. By sacrifice, Paul means yielding all you are and all you have to God in order to become like Christ and fulfill God's kingdom plan for your life. In so doing, you will be in sync with God's will for you.

2. *Submission.* God finds pleasure in the submission of

children to parents (Col. 3:20) and in the obedience of servants to their masters (Titus 2:9). As it is in the earthly economy, so it will be in the kingdom domain.

Your submission will not be in vain or without spiritual value. Look at this wonderful promise: "And whatever we ask we receive from Him, because we keep His commandments and do the things that are pleasing in His sight" (1 John 3:22).

3. *Walking in God's will.* Paul interceded for the Colossians with this wonderful prayer:

For this reason also, since the day we heard of it, we have not ceased to pray for you and to ask that you may be filled with the knowledge of His will in all spiritual wisdom and understanding, so that you may walk in a manner worthy of the Lord, to please Him in all respects, bearing fruit in every good work and increasing in the knowledge of God (Col. 1:9-10).

Transformation is central to Christianity. Being transformed into the likeness of Christ from the inside out. Like the caterpillar which becomes a lovely butterfly. "And do not be conformed to this world, but be transformed by the renewing of your mind, that you may prove what the will of God is, that which is good and acceptable and perfect" (Rom. 12:2).

4. *Spiritual focus.* The superlative spiritual aspect of being single lies in the opportunity to concentrate on the Lord without distractions from a spouse, children, and all the accompanying responsibilities of family life. "But I want you to be free from concern. One who is unmarried is concerned about the things of the Lord, how he may please the Lord" (1 Cor. 7:32).

This does not mean marriage is bad. Just the contrary, since the Bible says, "It is not good that the man should be alone" (Gen. 2:18, KJV). However, if you are single, God will use it for spiritual good, not social ill, because you have a kingdom advantage over your married counterpart. By application, even for us married folks, a spiritually focused life pleases God.

5. *Purity.* God wants us to become like Him. Because He is holy, He desires that we be holy too (1 Peter 1:16).

> *Brethren, we request and exhort you in the Lord Jesus that, as you received from us instruction as to how you ought to walk and please God (just as you actually do walk), that you may excel still more. For you know what commandments we gave you by the authority of the Lord Jesus. For this is the will of God, your sanctification; that is, that you abstain from sexual immorality (1 Thes. 4:1-3).*

Immorality abounds among Christians. It displeases our Heavenly Father to know we live lives that contain more darkness than light. To please God, we must flee immorality—like Joseph (Gen. 39:12; see also 1 Cor. 6:18).

A friend penned these significant words. I think of them often as a reminder that God wants me to reflect His purity.

> *My life is all Yours to shape as You will.*
> *I'll be the glove for Your hand to fill.*
> *I want to be pleasing to You. May it be,*
> *that You might be glorified somehow in me.* [2]

6. *Doing good.* It's so uncomplicated. "And do not neglect doing good and sharing; for with such sacrifices God is pleased" (Heb. 13:16).

The Philippians sent a gift to Paul by the hand of Epaphroditus. The apostle reports it pleased God (Phil. 4:18).

7. *Worship.* Praise, deeds of righteousness, and worship bring immense pleasure to God. Catch this repetitious idea in the Psalms:

> *I will praise the name of God with song, and shall magnify*

Him with thanksgiving. And it will please the Lord better than an ox or a young bull with horns and hoofs (Ps. 69:30-31).

Let them praise His name with dancing; let them sing praises to Him with timbrel and lyre. For the Lord takes pleasure in His people; He will beautify the afflicted ones with salvation (Ps. 149:3-4).

8. *Living in God's Spirit.* "Those who are in the flesh cannot please God" (Rom. 8:8; see also Gal. 5:16-17). It demands that we forsake our rights for the rights of God.

Therefore do not let what is for you a good thing be spoken of as evil; for the kingdom of God is not eating and drinking, but righteousness and peace and joy in the Holy Spirit. For he who in this way serves Christ is acceptable to God and approved by men (Rom. 14:16-18).

It means we act like Christ. "For even Christ did not please Himself; but as it is written, 'The reproaches of those who reproached Thee fell upon Me'" (Rom. 15:3).

9. *Preaching the truth.* When Paul preached, he did so to please God, not necessarily his audience (Gal. 1:10). Elsewhere he writes, "But just as we have been approved by God to be entrusted with the Gospel, so we speak, not as pleasing men but God, who examines our hearts" (1 Thes. 2:4).

All three persons of the Godhead are associated with truth — Father (John 3:33), Son (14:6), and Holy Spirit (16:13). To abandon truth is to abandon God. To compromise God's Word is to compromise God. With neither is God pleased (1 Cor. 1:20-21).

Fruitful Practitioners
With the many activities required and with this high level of spiritual demand, you might be asking, "Has anyone ever

brought pleasure to God?" Let me answer in the affirmative and give you some examples.

Enoch proved to be a man of faith, and he pleased God.

By faith Enoch was taken up so that he should not see death; and he was not found because God took him up; for he obtained the witness that before his being taken up he was pleasing to God. And without faith it is impossible to please Him, for he who comes to God must believe that He is, and that He is a rewarder of those who seek Him (Heb. 11:5-6).

As a young man, Solomon desired wisdom and truth more than riches. This pleased God. "And it was pleasing in the sight of the Lord that Solomon had asked this thing" (1 Kings 3:10).

Paul energetically reached out to please God. "Therefore also we have as our ambition, whether at home or absent, to be pleasing to Him" (2 Cor. 5:9).

Jesus testified to a lifestyle designed to please God. "And He who sent Me is with Me; He has not left Me alone, for I always do the things that are pleasing to Him" (John 8:29).

All of these men depended on God's Word for life direction and God's Spirit for a life dynamic. We have the same resources and the same opportunity for spiritually pleasing God.

Spiritual Payoffs

Making your priority in life to please God is not without its rewards. If you invest in God's pleasure, you will reap these divine dividends:

Peace .... "Glory to God in the highest, and on earth peace among men with whom He is pleased" (Luke 2:14).

Prayer Answered	"And whatever we ask we receive from Him, because we keep His commandments and do the things that are pleasing in His sight" (1 John 3:22).
Personal Relationships	"When a man's ways are pleasing to the Lord, He makes even his enemies to be at peace with him" (Prov. 16:7).

In the Academy Award-winning film *Chariots of Fire,* Eric Liddell, famed Olympian and missionary to China, conversed with his sister Jenny on a Scottish moor about the timing of his return to missionary work. His response remains etched in my memory. "I believe that God made me for a purpose—for China—but He also made me fast. And when I run I feel His pleasure."

What did God make you for? Do you sense His pleasure? Do you have God's pleasure as your highest ambition? Are you willing to put God's pleasure first?

Aim your life at the bull's-eye of God's pleasure and you will never miss the spiritual mark. You'll not be disappointed, and neither will God. Your heart will be filled with this great sense of commitment.

I rise up to worship, I stand to acclaim
The King of all ages, Christ Jesus His name.
I ask you, King Jesus, fulfill this desire,
Ignite me and make me, aflame and afire.
Come rule all my life,
Lord Jesus Christ, be Master and King.
Come rule all my life,
Lord Jesus Christ, be my everything.[3]

I will give thanks to Thee, O Lord my God,
with all my heart,
and will glorify Thy name forever.
Psalm 86:12

13
GLORIFYING GOD

It's fitting that I pen this concluding study during the Christmas season. The lyrics from so many carols speak of God's glory and fill our hearts with praise.

"Glory to God, all glory in the highest" comes from "O Come, All Ye Faithful" as does the line, "O Jesus, to Thee be all glory given." In "Hark the Herald Angels Sing," the angels shout out, "Glory to the newborn King." My favorite, however, remains the refrain from "Angels We Have Heard On High"—"Gloria in excelsis Deo." Glory to God in the highest!

After I preached one Sunday night, a young man inquired, "Since God's glory is complete, how can we possibly add anything to it? Why does Scripture command us to give Him glory?" We opened our Bibles to 2 Corinthians 3:18:

But we all, with unveiled face beholding as in a mirror the glory of the Lord, are being transformed into the same image from glory to glory, just as from the Lord, the Spirit.

I explained to him that by analogy God is to us as the sun is to the moon. As the sun is the exclusive source of light, so God is the sole source of glory; as the moon reflects light, so we reflect God's glory.

But because God's image in us was fractured by the Fall, sinful mankind refracts God's glory more than they perfectly reflect it back to Him. However, once we are transformed into the same image at the moment of salvation, we reflect more than we refract. Thus, God's glory is more and more returned to Him just as He transmitted it to us. That's how we can give to God something that He alone possesses and shares with no one (Isa. 42:8; 48:11).

God's glory dominates Scripture. Some have suggested "glory" as the Bible's unifying theme. Over 400 appearances of the word in Scripture support this thesis.

After studying every passage, it seems to me that from the perspective of, "What can I do to glorify God?" three distinct realms need to be identified and discussed. So I have listed the glorifying activities of a believer under these categories: (1) God directed, (2) Christian directed, and (3) unbeliever directed.

Upward Direction
Being God by definition includes being glorious. Many titles reflect God's glory:
- *The Lord of Glory (1 Cor. 2:8)*
- *The Majestic Glory (2 Peter 1:17)*
- *The King of Glory (Ps. 24:7-10)*
- *The Spirit of Glory (1 Peter 4:14)*
- *The Word of Glory (John 1:14)*

Most of God's glory reflected back to Him by us comes through acts of personal devotion and adoration that are God directed. Please note the activities of personal worship that glorify God.

1. *Living with purpose.* "Whether, then, you eat or drink or whatever you do, do all to the glory of God" (1 Cor. 10:31).

The famous eighteenth-century American preacher Jonathan Edwards applied this to his life by resolving, "That I will do whatsoever I think to be most to the glory of God." His resolve and yours frame the picture of life that is lived in all respects for God's glory. In so doing we will be an answer to Paul's prayer for the Philippians (1:9-11; see in contrast Dan. 5:23).

2. *Confessing sins.* "Then Joshua said to Achan, 'My son, I implore you, give glory to the Lord, the God of Israel, and give praise to Him; and tell me now what you have done. Do not hide it from me' " (Josh. 7:19).

To continue in sin shames God (Rev. 16:9). But to confess our sins acknowledges His holiness and brings Him glory.

3. *Praying expectantly.* "And whatever you ask in My name, that will I do, that the Father may be glorified in the Son" (John 14:13).

Your prayers in Christ's name bring the Father glory. Let's begin our prayers with Moses' petition, "I pray Thee, show me Thy glory" (Ex. 33:18).

4. *Living purely.* "Flee immorality. Every other sin that a man commits is outside the body, but the immoral man sins against his own body. Or do you not know that your body is a temple of the Holy Spirit who is in you, whom you have from God, and that you are not your own? For you have been bought with a price: therefore glorify God in your body" (1 Cor. 6:18-20).

It glorifies God to live in the light of His holy character.

5. *Submitting to Christ.* "Therefore also God highly exalted Him, and bestowed on Him the name which is above every name, that at the name of Jesus every knee should bow, of those who are in heaven, and on earth, and under the earth, and that every tongue should confess that Jesus Christ is Lord, to the glory of God the Father" (Phil. 2:9-11).

6. *Praising God.* "For all things are for your sakes, that the

grace which is spreading to more and more people may cause the giving of thanks to abound to the glory of God" (2 Cor. 4:15).

The Samaritan healed of leprosy glorified God with praise as did the angels at Christ's birth (Luke 17:18, 2:14). Let your mouth be filled with the Lord's praise and glory all day long (Ps. 71:8).

7. *Obeying God.* "Because of the proof given by this ministry they will glorify God for your obedience to your confession of the Gospel of Christ, and for the liberality of your contribution to them and to all" (2 Cor. 9:13).

8. *Growing in faith.* "Yet, with respect to the promise of God, he [Abraham] did not waver in unbelief, but grew strong in faith, giving glory to God, and being fully assured that what He had promised, He was able also to perform" (Rom. 4:20-21).

9. *Suffering for Christ's sake.* "By no means let any of you suffer as a murderer, or thief, or evildoer, or a troublesome meddler; but if anyone suffers as a Christian, let him not feel ashamed, but in that name let him glorify God" (1 Peter 4:15-16).

Peter knew of what he wrote, for years earlier Christ had told him by what kind of death he would glorify God (John 21:19).

10. *Rejoicing in God.* "Glory in His holy name; let the heart of those who seek the Lord be glad" (1 Chron. 16:10).

11. *Worshiping God.* "All nations whom Thou hast made shall come and worship before Thee, O Lord; and they shall glorify Thy name" (Ps. 86:9).

12. *Bearing spiritual fruit.* "By this is My Father glorified, that you bear much fruit, and so prove to be My disciples" (John 15:8).

Inward Dimension

The Christian life begins by being right with God, but it does not end there. From the upward direction, we now turn inward to ways that believers can glorify God in the church and among themselves.

The catchy note that follows captures the normal process in the church. However, we know that whatever is accomplished goes to the credit and glory of God, who has everything to do with spiritual victories (Eph. 3:20-21).

There are six stages in all great projects. First there is enthusiasm. Next comes doubt. This is followed by panic. Phase four is the search for the guilty . . . then punishment of the innocent. The final stage? Giving credit to those who didn't have anything to do with it. [1]

13. *Proclaiming God's Word.* "Finally, brethren, pray for us that the word of the Lord may spread rapidly and be glorified, just as it did also with you" (2 Thes. 3:1).

14. *Serving God's people.* "As each one has received a special gift, employ it in serving one another, as good stewards of the manifold grace of God. Whoever speaks, let him speak, as it were, the utterances of God; whoever serves, let him do so as by the strength which God supplies; so that in all things God may be glorified through Jesus Christ, to whom belongs the glory and dominion forever and ever. Amen" (1 Peter 4:10-11).

15. *Purifying Christ's church.* "That He might present to Himself the church in all her glory, having no spot or wrinkle or any such thing; but that she should be holy and blameless" (Eph. 5:27).

16. *Giving sacrificially.* "Because of the proof given by this ministry they will glorify God for your obedience to your confession of the Gospel of Christ, and for the liberality of your contribution to them and to all" (2 Cor. 9:13).

17. *Unifying believers.* "And the glory which Thou hast given Me I have given them; that they may be one, just as We are one" (John 17:22).

As Christ accepted us, so we are to accept one another to God's glory (Rom. 15:7).

Outward Dynamic

First up, then in, and now out. That completes the cycle.
Someone may ask, "Which of these three is most important?" Let me respond with a question, "What leg on a three-
legged stool is most important?" All are equally important,
but the order in which we glorify God is crucial. We must
first be fixed on Him before we can minister to one another.
Then, unless we are right in the body of Christ, we can never
hope to reach out to the lost with the Gospel of Christ.

18. *Salvation of the lost.* "His glory is great through Thy
salvation, splendor and majesty Thou dost place upon him"
(Ps. 21:5).

"To the praise of His glory" dominates Paul's comments
on salvation (Eph. 1:6, 12, 14). It proved that way in the
salvation of Paul (Gal. 1:23-24) and Cornelius (Acts 11:18).
Since the lost have fallen short of God's glory (Rom. 3:23),
then to be saved is to have that glory restored.

19. *Shining Christ's light.* "Let your light shine before men
in such a way that they may see your good works, and glorify
your Father who is in heaven" (Matt. 5:16).

20. *Spreading God's Gospel.* "For all things are for your
sakes, that the grace which is spreading to more and more
people may cause the giving of thanks to abound to the glory
of God" (2 Cor. 4:15).

This proved to be Paul's experience on his first missionary
journey. When the Gentiles heard the Gospel, they rejoiced,
glorified God, and believed (Acts 13:48).

A converted Hindu addressing a number of his countrymen
once said, "I am by birth of an insignificant and contemptible
caste, so low that if a Brahman should chance to touch me he
must go and bathe in the Ganges for the purpose of purification; and yet God has been pleased to call me not merely to a
knowledge of the Gospel, but to the high office of teaching it
to others. My friends," said the converted Hindu, "do you
know the reason of God's comfort? It is this: If God had
selected one of you learned Brahmans and made you a

preacher, on becoming successful in making converts, by-standers would have said it was an amazing learning of the Brahman and his great weight of character that were the cause; but now, when anyone is convinced by my instrumentality, no one thinks of ascribing any praise to me; and God, as is His due, has all the glory."[2]

A Concluding Comment

Ichabod, which means "no glory" in Hebrew, would be the worst thing imaginable for a believer (1 Sam. 4:21). For God's glory to be absent from a believer or the church is unthinkable. The glory of God needs to be our consuming quest.

The initial question is asked in *The Shorter Catechism,* "What is the chief end of man?" Answer: "Man's chief end is to glorify God, and to enjoy Him forever." The ultimate object of our thoughts and priorities should be the glory of God. Our total being should be absorbed by this thrilling prospect which is the pinnacle experience of spiritual intimacy.

I've often marveled at a commemorative sign which stands in front of a building complex devoted to ministry. It captures the "shoe leather" sense of glorifying God. The plaque reads:

ARROWHEAD SPRINGS VILLAGE

DONATED BY FIVE BUSINESSMEN WHO WANT TO GIVE GOD *ALL* THE GLORY

So, like these men, let the beatitude of the psalmist and the doxology of Paul be yours now and forever more.

Blessed be the Lord God, the God of Israel, who alone works wonders. And blessed be His glorious name forever; and may the whole earth be filled with His glory. Amen, and Amen (Ps. 72:18-19).

Now to our God and Father be the glory forever and ever. Amen (Phil. 4:20).

NOTES

INTRODUCTION
1. Quoted by Albert M. Wells, Jr. in *Inspiring Quotations* (Nashville: Thomas Nelson Publishers, 1988), p. 121.

2. Gordon MacDonald, *Restoring Your Spiritual Passion* (Nashville: Oliver-Nelson Books, 1986), pp. 10-11.

STEP ONE—"GETTING ACQUAINTED"
1. Carl F.H. Henry, "Evangelical Courage in an Age of Darkness," *Table Talk*, 14:1 (January, 1990), pp. 11-12.

ONE—KNOWING GOD
1. Gordon Verrell, "Hershiser Closer to History," in *Long Beach Press-Telegram* (Sept. 25, 1988), C5.

2. A.W. Tozer, *The Pursuit of God* (Harrisburg, Pa.: Christian Publications, Inc., 1948), pp. 14-15.

3. Philip Yancey, "Ghandi and Christianity" in *Christianity Today* (April 8, 1983), p. 16.

4. Max Wertheimer, *How a Rabbi Found Peace* (Lansing, Ill.: American Messianic Fellowship, n.d.), pp. 2, 3, 7, 11.

5. Myra Brooks Welch, "The Touch of the Master's Hand" in *The Treasury of Religious Verse* (Westwood, N.J.: Fleming H. Revell Co., 1962), pp. 87-88.

6. Jon Mohr, "A Note From The Composer" in *He Holds The Keys* (Chatsworth, Calif.: The Sparrow Corporation, 1987). International copyright secured. All rights reserved. Used by permission.

TWO—LISTENING TO GOD
1. Larry Crabb, "Facing the Pain in Relationships," *Discipleship Journal*, 43(1988), p. 16.

2. Published by Fleming H. Revell.

3. For further insturciton on how to use these practical steps for fruitful Bible study, see Richard Mayhue, *How to Interpret the Bible for Yourself* (Winona Lake, Ind.: BMH Books, 1989).

THREE—THINKING LIKE GOD
1. Jim Downing, *Meditation* (Colorado Springs, Colo.: NavPress, 1976), pp. 7-8.

2. Hary Blamires, *The Christian Mind* (Ann Arbor, Mich. : Servant Books, 1963), pp. 110-111.

3. Richard Mayhue, *Unmasking Satan* (Wheaton, Ill.: Victor Books, 1988), p. 21.

4. Charles Colson, *Against the Night* (Ann Arbor, Mich.: Servant Publications, 1989), pp. 26-27.

FOUR—LISTENING TO GOD
1. Ray Stedman, *Jesus Teaches on Prayer* (Waco, Texas: Word Books, 1975), p. 7.

2. A.T. Pierson quoted by John MacArthur, Jr. in *Grace To You* (January, 1983), p. 1.

STEP TWO—"GROWING TOGETHER"
1. John Newton, *John Newton* (Chicago: Moody Press, n.d.), p. 159.

SIX—PRAISING GOD
1. *Grace to You* (June/July, 1985), p. 8.

2. See Nathan Stone, *Names of God* (Chicago: Moody Press, 1944) for an expanded discussion.

SEVEN—GIVING TO GOD
1. Clovis Chappell in *Christian Medical Society Journal.* VII: 4 (Fall, 1976), p. 1.

2. Ron Blue in *Discipleship Journal,* 9:5 (September/October, 1989), p. 20.

EIGHT—PURSUING GOD
1. Affirmed by Gary Collins, *The Rebuilding of Psychology* (Wheaton, Ill.: Tyndale House Publishers, 1977), pp. 73-92.

2. Bruce Shelley, "Justin: Witness and Martyr" in *Moody Monthly* (June, 1986), p. 27.

3. Dallas Willard, "Discipleship for Super-Christians Only?" in *Christianity Today* (October 10, 1980), p. 23.

4. Don Hescott, "A Lesson on Commitment from a Communist," in *Masterpiece* (September/October, 1989), p. 24.

5. Oscar Broneer, "The Apostle Paul and the Isthmian Games," in *The Biblical Archaeologist.* XXV:1 (February, 1962), p. 17.

6. Used by permission.

7. Contained in *The Treasury of Religious Verse* (Westwood, N.J.: Fleming H. Revell, 1962).

STEP THREE—"GOING FOR BROKE"
1. Norman Grubb, *C.T. Studd: Cricketeer and Pioneer* (Fort Washington, Pa.: Christian Literature Crusade, 1982), p. 3.

NINE—KNOWING GOD'S WILL

1. Quoted by Philip Yancey in *Christianity Today* (Sept. 16, 1983), p. 27.
2. Quoted in *Famous Last Words,* compiled by Jonathon Green (London: Omnibus Press, 1979), p. 28.

TEN—FINDING GOD'S WILL

1. Elisabeth Elliot, *Shadow of the Almighty* (Grand Rapids, Mich.: Zondervan Publishing House, 1958), p. 128.
2. Gary Inrig, *Hearts of Iron, Feet of Clay* (Chicago: Moody Press, 1979), pp. 116-117.
3. Paul Little, *Affirming the Will of God* (Downers Grove, Ill.: InterVarsity Press, 1971), pp. 17-18.
4. T.S. Rendall, "The Lord Led Me—But Did He?" in *The Prairie Overcomer* (May, 1982), p. 201.
5. John Flavel quoted by Sinclair Ferguson, in "The Task of Seeking God's Mysterious Will," *Eternity* (May, 1988), p. 25.
6. Used by permission of Dr. Homer Kent, Jr., then President of Grace Theological Seminary.
7. Paul L. Tan, *Encyclopedia of 7,700 Illustrations* (Rockville, Md.: Assurance Publishers, 1979), p. 738.

ELEVEN—GRASPING GOD'S GREATNESS

1. Used by permission.
2. Charles R. Swindoll, *Come Before Winter* (Portland, Ore.: Multnomah Press, 1985), pp. 294-295.
3. Jerry Bergman, "The Pinnacle of Divine Creativity," in *Ministry* (November, 1984), pp. 28-29.
4. Used by permission.
5. Howard A. Snyder, *The Radical Wesley* (Grand Rapids, Mich.: Francis Asbury Press, 1980), p. 92.

TWELVE—PLEASING GOD

1. Used by permission of LAFD Deputy Chief Dave Parsons.
2. Music and lyrics by Don Kistler (Yucaipa, Calif.: Oak Tree Music, 1979). Used by permission of the composer.
3. Author unknown.

THIRTEEN—GLORIFYING GOD

1. Unknown author quoted by Charles Swindoll, *Newsbreak* (November 13, 1988), p. 4.
2. Author unknown.